THE COMIC IMAGE OF THE JEW
Explorations of a Pop Culture Phenomenon

THE COMIC IMAGE OF THE JEW

Explorations of a Pop Culture Phenomenon

Sig Altman

Rutherford • Madison • Teaneck
Fairleigh Dickinson University Press

© 1971 by Sig Altman
Library of Congress Catalogue Card Number: 71-146161

Associated University Presses, Inc.
Cranbury, New Jersey 08512

The author wishes to thank:

Simon & Schuster, Inc., for permission to quote from Bruce Jay Friedman, *Stern*. Copyright © 1962 by Bruce Jay Friedman. Reprinted by permission of Simon & Schuster, Inc.

The Viking Press, Inc., for permission to quote from *The Price* by Arthur Miller. Copyright © 1968 by Arthur Miller & Ingeborg M. Miller, Trustee. All rights reserved. Reprinted by permission of The Viking Press, Inc.

ISBN: 0-8386-7869-6
Printed in the United States of America

For Jill

For Jill

CONTENTS

Acknowledgments	9
Introduction	11
On Method	21

I
The Media and the Jewish Comic Image 29

Introduction	31
Films	33
Theatre	51
Television	71
Books	100
Summary of Media Survey	119

II
The Historical Background of the Jewish Comic Image 121

Introduction	123
The Humor of Early Times	125
The Humor of Emancipation	135
The Humor of Non-Emancipation	146
The Humor of the Cities	159
The Humor of the Anti-Semites	172

III
183

The Humor of the Jewish Comedian	185
Conclusion	197
Appendix	206
Bibliography	218
Index	225

ACKNOWLEDGMENTS

I take this opportunity to thank Professor F. William Howton, of The City University of New York, who encouraged some earlier work of mine in the analysis of popular culture. My thanks are also due to the following currently on the Graduate Faculty of Political and Social Science of the New School for Social Research, where the present work evolved to serve as basis for a doctoral dissertation: Professor Stanley Diamond, for his approval and encouragement of this project, Professor Samuel E. Stern, for some fruitful suggestions concerning the structure of the text, and Professors Urs Jaeggi, Solomon Miller, Benjamin Nelson, Emil Oestereicher, Bernard Rosenberg, and Arthur J. Vidich, for their interest and for some stimulating discussions. The responsibility for whatever shortcomings still inhere in this work is of course mine alone.

I thank the following for permission to quote from copyrighted material:

Jerome Agel, for excerpts from "Cocktail Party," in *Books*.

Commentary, for excerpts from Alfred Kazin, "The Jew as Modern Writer."

Crown Publishers, for excerpts from Sholom Aleichem, *The Old Country*.

Douglas Book Corporation, for excerpts from *The Essential Lenny Bruce*.

The Jewish Publication Society, for excerpts from Israel Abrahams, *Jewish Life in the Middle Ages*.

Harold Ober Associates, Incorporated, for excerpts from Gregor von Rezzori, "Memoirs of an Anti-Semite," © 1969 by The New Yorker Magazine, Inc.

Random House, Inc., for excerpts from Philip Roth, *Portnoy's Complaint*, and from John Updike, *Bech: A Book*.

Schocken Books, Inc., for excerpts from Hans Bach, *Jüdische Memoiren aus drei Jahrhunderten*, Schocken Verlag, Berlin.

Simon & Schuster, Inc., for excerpts from Bruce Jay Friedman, *Stern*.

The Viking Press, Inc., for excerpts from Saul Bellow, *Herzog*.

INTRODUCTION

This study was prompted, or at least triggered, by a fleeting incident witnessed some time in the late sixties on a television "talk" show. An interviewee, in the course of a totally serious discussion, made the quite serious remark, "I looked it up in the Jewish Encyclopedia." There immediately followed a burst of laughter from the studio audience, which obviously sensed a joke about to materialize, or perhaps saw one already born. The laughter rather suddenly subsided, however, as the collective realization apparently dawned that no joke was in fact intended at all. Nevertheless, the comic quality of the word "Jewish" in the public consciousness had been perfectly demonstrated.

This small incident produces in actual experience what usually can only be conceived in theory: a limiting case, a logical extreme. For according to the contention of this study that the image of the Jew is, in the entertainment media and by extension in the public eye, a comic one, it must logically follow that even the very word "Jewish" has become laden with humorous overtones. This supposition would be difficult to prove normally from audience reactions on television, for example, since the occasional serious contexts for the word "Jewish" are likely to be quite unambiguous and the audience, forewarned, is therefore not likely to be trapped in inappropriate laughter. In the "Encyclopedia" incident, however, the discussion preceding the crucial remark had in fact not been about anything Jewish, so that when that remark finally came the word "Jewish" stood in a kind of no man's land: a solemn context had not been specifically prepared for it, but neither had there been comedy. The audience laughed nevertheless.

Besides demonstrating the "Jewish comic image" in action, the Encyclopedia incident also helps illuminate the implications of such an image. Is a group that is primarily laughed at, or laughed about, being maligned or "oppressed," or is it being "loved" or even admired? In this case, the audience demonstrates of course that it is conditioned, at the very least, not to take the Jew seriously: he is simply not on a par with whatever connotations of seriousness inhere, for example, in the word *encyclopedia*. He is not quite "legitimate." This collective frame of mind seems hardly compatible with affirmative feelings, let alone admiration.

The use of the currently fashionable word *image* to denote emotional and/or intellectual impact on a crowd implies the view that collective perception results in the formation of something as rich and complex as a picture, rather than merely an "opinion" easily translatable into a phrase or sentence. If this study thus concerns itself with the *image* of the Jew, it does so in an attempt to examine a phenomenon that has not significantly shown up on the relevant surveys of public opinion. Yet, at the same time, the basic contention concerning the existence of a Jewish comic image is based upon evidence that is

INTRODUCTION

very much available and really inescapable for any "consumer" of the media. It may in fact be suspected that the comic image of the American Jew in TV, films, theatre, and popular books, has become one of those everyday, taken-for-granted social facts that one can hardly see for their very proximity to the observer. For that very reason alone it may perhaps be useful to attempt an analysis of the content of today's mass media relative to the Jewish image. Such a project might at least make the obvious somewhat more apparent.

That the mass media reflect and, in turn, reinforce public opinion is axiomatic in mass communication studies. That the mass media may furthermore highlight aspects of the public consciousness that will not so readily show up in opinion surveys is perhaps a less heavily emphasized point in those studies, yet there is the sociology-of-literature tradition, which includes not only such Marxist analyses of the implicit content of "high literature" as those of Lukacs and Goldmann, but also depth studies of popular literature such as those by Leo Lowenthal, or of popular films by Siegfried Kracauer and by Wolfman and Leites. While the latter, however, aim at unearthing generally hidden or disguised types of content that require a rather formidable apparatus of interpretation, the content to be isolated and analyzed here will be found to be quite easily accessible, and very explicit. Certainly, the comic image of the Jew in the media should be demonstrable without the need to interpret obscure meanings.

It may be asked why it is—if the content to be analyzed does indeed, as is assumed, reflect the public consciousness and is at the same time on the surface—that it does not tend to show up on public opinion surveys. One answer might be that, because of its complex emotional character, the kind of consciousness involved becomes visible only within the broad framework of the popular arts. A random look at some polls quoted in a compilation issued by the American Jewish Committee (96) makes this point clear. On page 63, for example, the survey question is "In what ways are Jews different?" The two most frequently given answers cited are: 1) "Their religion (church, belief) is different." 2) "They are rich, shrewd, successful in business." These answers are followed by others, none of which is "They are funny (comic, ridiculous)." It becomes understandable on looking at the results of such polls that this kind of answer would not be readily on a respondent's tongue since it would be an answer somehow incompatible with the mental "set" evoked by the questionnaire. At the same time it would not necessarily be incompatible with any of the answers quoted.

It might be appropriate here to touch briefly on just how a "comic image" of a group might be related to the attitudes concerning that group, as elicited by opinion surveys. Following generally accepted psychological assumptions concerning humor as a means of channeling blocked aggression, one might interpret persistent laughter in relation to a group as the behavioral equivalent of negative attitudes, as already suggested. If that is the case then the comic image is a form of "acting out" of what the surveys register in sober language, and nothing more. And if that is the case the comic image has already been thoroughly covered by the surveys. However, it is difficult to posit such a direct relationship between comic image and recorded attitude simply because of the fact that, while the Jewish comic image has gained in visibility, anti-Jewish attitudes have markedly declined in the surveys over the last 25 years (96, p. 210; 90, pp. 16–18). Must it then be assumed after all that a comic image is *not* really indicative of hostility? Since this image is, as far as the media go, largely a creation of Jews themselves, one might think that this is so. However, as will be shown later, Jewish humor has traveled in time a road leading as far as outright self-rejection. The Jewish source of the Jewish image in the media is thus no proof of its non-hostile intent, or effect. But neither is the "officially" charted decline in anti-Semitism itself necessarily such proof. The report appended to the evidence of this decline (96) in fact refers to the possibility of a persisting latency of anti-Jewish attitudes, which does not register in opinion polls.

Conceivably, it is precisely such latencies that a comic image of a group reflects. For the circumscribed and self-aware occasion of responding to an interview or questionnaire, the media substitute the offguard situation of an audience facing a performance and reacting spontaneously out of its entire reservoir of available dispositions. An "ideal" situation of this kind was observed of course in the Jewish Encyclopedia incident, in which the television medium clearly demonstrated in what manner its audience is itself "programmed."

The behavior of the audience in that incident suggests, as was said earlier, a development of the public consciousness to the point where the word "Jewish," uttered on a bland occasion, has become a stimulus to which the automatic response is laughter. There are numerous examples of the commercial exploitation of this phenomenon, such as the "You don't have to be Jewish . . ." bread campaign, or the appearance of a comic best-seller entitled simply *How To Be A Jewish Mother* (37), followed, after its success, by a humorous book that even more clearly demonstrates the comic possibilities of the word "Jewish": its title is *What's A Jewish Girl?* (98).

But the association of the Jew with humor spreads beyond the confines of this narrow exploitation. In the course of what has been termed a "Jewish Renaissance," a great number of novels, plays, and films with Jewish content have appeared over the last few years and, as will be shown, the prevailing image of the Jew in this large output is a comic one. In the *New York Times Book Review* of September 1, 1968, a reviewer of a new Jewish novel characterizes this "renaissance" as "a form of self-exploitation that bears the same relation to Jewish identity that Stepin Fetchit once did to the Negro: lots of laughs—see Sammy Schlemiel Hate Himself in Public."

Not always has there existed a Jewish image, comic or otherwise, in the media. Thus, in July 1952 an article in *Commentary* by Henry Popkin, significantly entitled "The Vanishing Jew of Our Popular Culture" (73), describes "the great retreat" after the early thirties. Popkin shows that the twenties did not tend to hide the existence of the Jew, but that during the early thirties "the American answer to the banishment of the Jews from public life in Germany was the banishment of Jewish figures from the popular arts in the United States." For example, "in the Avon Books reprint of Irving Shulman's novel of juvenile delinquency in Brooklyn, *The Amboy Dukes,* every trace of Jewish reference is eliminated. Bar Mitzvah becomes 'confirmation,' . . . Goldfarb becomes Abbot, Samuel becomes Saunders, etc." Or Arthur Miller subjects his plays *All My Sons* and *Death of a Salesman* to "pre-censorship" by carefully "dejudaizing" his characters. Or in the 1941 film version of Ben Hecht's 1931 play *Front Page,* the

Governor's emissary Irving Pincus becomes Joe Pettibone. Or Samson is identified only as a member of the "tribe of Dan." As far as Hollywood is concerned, Popkin concludes, anno 1952, that "the idea that the Jews simply are *there* in the community" is a "revolutionary idea."

Observing the reappearance of the Jewish figure in the media, one must assume that this sense of peril has abated, or even disappeared. Yet there are other factors making for this reappearance and among these a rather important, though apparently fortuitous one, seems to be the introduction into American pop culture (in the early fifties) of nationwide televised informal talk. Since the daily schedule required a great supply of "personalities" to be shown talking (and performing as well) the networks began to draw, among others, on many a Jewish comedian who had hitherto been seen only by the patrons of nightclubs and Catskill hotels. These comedians had developed their styles with a view to their limited and specialized audiences whose demands, because of the nightclub's "heightened" occasion and cover charge, or the Catskill hotels' "in-group" atmosphere, were assumed to be for experiences not then available on the media, including a more open approach to the publicly "risqué" subject of Jewishness. As these Jewish comedians began to appear on television, they retained their "in" style—i.e. their Jewishness—because they presumably could only be what they already were; because, in view of the declining evidence of anti-Semitism, the pressure on the part of the media to tone down or eliminate anything Jewish must have begun to wane; and because the "shock" alone of a hitherto "tabu" subject produced laughter.

If the Jewish comedian thus is the spearhead of the Jewish return to the media, he may also be responsible for setting the tone for the prevailing humorousness of most things Jewish in the media. It might nevertheless seem far-fetched, for example, to attribute Philip Roth's impulse to write of Jewish experience in the comic mode to his being influenced by the ubiquitous Jewish comedian. (Though the form of "stand-up" comic monologue and the "stand-up" device of pervasive hyperbole employed in *Portnoy's Complaint* (83) by a narrator who is, incidentally, supposed to be lying down, might tempt one to make such a connection). But the Jewish comedian is certainly the central figure of the Jewish comic image and its "purest" exemplification: his is as standard a role in the entertainment world as the Italian Tenor and the Negro Boxer. Moreover, Jewish Comedian is the *only* explicitly Jewish role in the media.

This close association between comedy and Jewishness might seem to become understandable when one considers that, after all, *the* classic writer of the Jews in modern times is Sholem Aleichem, a comic writer. There obviously must be something in the situation of the Jew in the world that results in the emergence of humor. The Jewish comedian, one might say, is in that tradition. However, the difficulty in this explanation lies in the drastic difference between the situation of the Jew in America today and that of the Jew in Sholem Aleichem's Russia. That difference is pointed up, for example, by Will Herberg. (47) His analysis shows that being a Jew in this country means essentially being a member of one of the three faiths that constitute the "triple melting pot," in which the diverse ethnic attributes of immigrants are dissolved and an American identity is formed. This is a point of view not seriously disputed in social science and borne out recently, for example, in a study of Jews in Providence by Goldstein-Goldscheider. (33)

If Herberg's view has validity, as is assumed, it is a view difficult to reconcile with the thriving comic image of the Jew. To be sure, the growth in "leveling" of the three major faiths might account for a diminished Jewish timorousness and a greater willingness to place oneself in view of all who care to look. But it would not account for the *comic* image. However, the interpretation of this image as a manifestation of *latent* hostility might at first sight not seem to be irreconcilable with the Herberg thesis. There seems in fact to be considerable persuasiveness in the argument that, with American Jewish respectability becoming comparable to that of Protestants and Catholics, anti-Jewish feelings flow increasingly into covert, "disreputable" channels such as laughter. Yet such reasoning, on closer view, is contradictory. The very meaning of "triple melting pot" is that not only can the American Jew be as American as the members of the two other major faiths, but that he can also be as Jewish as they are Protestant or Catholic. But if the Jewish comic image is thought of, for example, in terms of the Encyclopedia incident on TV, it becomes rather clear that to be a Jewish American is simply not so "easy" as it is to be a Protestant or a Catholic one. In fact, the comic image of the Jew—created largely by himself yet perpetuated in the public consciousness—turns out on closer inspection to constitute evidence, as well as reinforcement, of the fact that Jewishness is *not* really respectable in America.

It might still be argued that the Jewish comic image should not make it difficult to accept Herberg's point of view, since according to that view the leveling of the three religions becomes possible only after a gradual sloughing off and disappearance of ethnic characteristics over a number of generations. Might then not a lingering "ethnicity" in American Jewish identity account for that comic image? Again, the argument is less than plausible if one juxtaposes a necessarily diminishing ethnicity with (as will be shown) a *flourishing* comic image. What is perhaps more important, the nature of that comic image is not primarily ethnic: dialect comedy has nearly disappeared; the jokes turn generally on *Bar Mitzvah* rather than the old country, on the rabbi rather than the greenhorn. Here, in fact, is an essentially "religious" humor, which finds its apotheosis in Jackie Mason, whose publicity proclaims him as a rabbi-turned-comedian, or in Alan King's impersonation of a rabbi giving a *comic* funeral oration (in the film *Bye Bye Braverman*), an instance of the comedian-turned-rabbi-turned-comedian.

It seems then that a Jewish comic image is difficult to reconcile with the prevailing sociological view of Jewish life in American society. Yet casual observation is sufficient to confirm that such an image indeed seems to exist. What this study consequently sets out to do is, first, to validate the assumption concerning the existence of that image in the media, and second, to explore, and possibly understand, the apparently contradictory fact of its existence by examining the meaning and function of humor in the Jewish past.

ON METHOD

The research will be divided into two major parts, the first dealing with the humor concerning Jews in the popular culture, and the second with the role of humor in Jewish history. A third part will be devoted to an "impression" of the Jewish comedian.

The purpose of the popular culture (or mass media) study is to ascertain the existence of a comic image of the Jew, and in addition to determine the nature of that image. That is to say, the attempt will be made not only to assess whether popular subject matter in films, books, theatre, and television, as it relates to Jews, is generally rendered in terms of comedy, but also what the "tone" of that comedy is and to what extent, if any, that comedy is a reflection of the actual situation of the Jews in American society.

The fundamental assumption behind this assessment of the mass media will be that the old American tradition of ethnic humor was and is "valid" in the sense that it reflects the idiosyncrasy of the outsider as perceived by the insider, and that it furthermore serves to relieve the stress of the conflict often inherent in the encounter of different, especially competing, ethnic groups. In this way the life situation of a minority group member is a "natural" subject for comedy, with the comic predicaments of a situation thus depicted arising directly out of the comic hero's ethnically distinct or "strange" identity. Such a relationship becomes clear if one refers to such a standard comic convention as the mother-in-law joke. The comedy grows out of the specific relationship of tension between mother-in-law and son-in-law. The mother-in-law joke would be no joke if the comedy were made to derive from some random quirk of the mother-in-law heroine that had nothing to do with that relationship.

Similarly, the ethnic joke, the joke about specific groups, exists by virtue of inter-group tensions. For example, the idea of Scottish stinginess, often used as the basis of jokes about Scotsmen, crystallized only as a result of the encounter between the Scots and the English; in Scotland itself there are of course both stingy and non-stingy Scots. There are, however, different ways in which inter-ethnic confrontation may be reflected in humor. For instance, the actual clash itself may become the basic comic predicament. An example is the play *Jacobowsky and the Colonel* by Franz Werfel, in which a nationalistic Polish aristocrat is thrown together during World War II with a cosmopolitan Jew skilled in the art of survival. Idiosyncrasy dominates behavior on either side: privileged arrogance here, underprivileged slipperiness there. Such direct depiction of the clash between privileged and non-privileged may be typical of the approach of the non-privileged to the comedy of inter-group tension; Chaplin's comedy comes to mind as another example. On the other hand, the privileged, or insider, group tends not to depict such direct encounter, finding it beneath its own dignity, as it were, to include itself in the joke. Its humor therefore will focus only on the idiosyncrasies associated with the outsider and attributed to him in *all* his actions, even when he is acting "intramurally," with his own kind. (Example: A Scotsman's wife is dying. The husband is at the bedside, but has to leave the room. He says to his wife, before leaving, "If you feel yourself slipping, Maggie, don't forget to blow out the candle.") The outsiders, in turn, may tell these jokes about themselves to each other, especially if they begin to identify with the insiders' point-of-view. Thus, a Jew may tell another Jew a more or less self-denigrating joke about two other Jews.

Above, the "validity" of ethnic humor was made dependent upon the condition that its content reflect an actual state of inter-group tension, as well as on its tendency to mitigate that tension. It is possible, though, for ethnic humor to reflect such tension at the same time that it attempts not to mitigate but intensify it. This is the case with explicit anti-Semitic humor. The process by which hostility is displaced by laughter is here reversed: laughter leads, or is meant to lead, to intensified hostility. Still there might be a basis even here for what was called the validity of ethnic humor. For example, the Jewish specialization in money-lending during one period of European history could become the basis of a cartoon showing a Jew counting gleefully a mountain of coins while his wife sits miserably waiting for him to come to bed. During the Nazi era, however, and at some earlier periods as well, anti-Semitic humor might be said to have lost all such validity as ethnic humor, since *all* evil was attributed to Jews and it became possible to symbolize that evil, embodied by the nose in the shape of the figure six, in any and all contexts, *or no context at all,* with the expectation of a conditioned hostile response. That kind of "humor" no longer reflected in its content the *reality* of inter-group tension.

In assessing, then, the character of the Jewish comic image in the popular culture, these distinctions concerning the various types of relationship possible between such an image and reality will be kept in mind. The "ultimate" comic image, the Jewish Comic Image in capitals, would, according to the above considerations, be one that is devoid of "valid" ethnic humor. This would be the case in comedy where Jewishness constitutes a gratuitous element of the humor, associated with no social reality other than the presumed capacity for Jewishness to produce laughter. Example: Show the adventures of a comic American stumblebum and give him the name of Irving Goldfarb. Such a ploy would represent use of the Jewish Comic Image.

In examining the mass media materials, an attempt will be made to obtain a correct overall impression, in relation to the problem at hand, of films, books, plays, and television of recent vintage (i.e. approximately the six years leading up to Summer 1970). This attempt will not entail only a quantitative approach, since, as indicated, what is being asked is not only "How much?" but also "What kind?" The hypothesis of a Jewish Comic Image, as defined above, would stand confirmed only if, first, the overall image of the Jew is more comic than that of any other group (this means that, in case of a fairly large number of items for each group, the relation of comic to serious items is higher in the case of Jews than in the case of other groups, as well as that the total of humorous items about Jews is higher than the total of any other group); second, the humor pertaining to Jews is primarily of the "arbitrary" kind. Establishing the second point, especially, entails rather detailed analysis of content—a "qualitative" procedure to which Berelson, in his book on content analysis (10), assigns an honored place in social research. Though a danger of bias may arise in connection with such interpretive methods, the kind of analysis envisioned can, and indeed must, be self-validating if whatever conclusions reached are shown to derive logically from the data presented and discussed.

The guidebook to this projected tour of a section of cultural landscape will consist most importantly of newspaper and periodical reviews of plays and films, of best-seller lists, and of direct acquaintance with the material. For the survey of television, several evening talk shows, probably the most topical and also "spontaneous" genre of TV presentations, will be monitored systematically over given periods.

Pertaining to the second section, dealing with the role of humor in the Jewish past, it is intended to trace the changes in the nature and content of that humor alongside changes in history. In this way some clarification might emerge for the understanding of the changing functions humor may perform for a group as the social-historical situation changes. As a consequence, the relation between Jewish humor and the present American situation may be laid bare. Jewish humor emanating from non-Jewish sources will also be looked at, in order to ascertain a connection between it and humor from Jewish sources. Standard histories will be used in this section alongside various collections of Jewish humor, from early times to recent.

The two sections previewed above, the media analysis and the historical survey, while separate studies, are of course closely related. The first section will attempt to establish the existence of a "problem," the second to trace it back in time to its source, if possible, and thus, conceivably, move toward its explanation.

A third section, finally, will consist of a chapter on the Jewish Comedian, who is the foremost exponent of American Jewish humor and at the same time the link to the humor of the Jewish past, where his cultural equivalent appears rather early.

THE COMIC IMAGE
OF THE JEW
Explorations of a Pop Culture Phenomenon

I
The Media
and the Jewish Comic Image

INTRODUCTION

THE MEDIA ANALYZED IN THIS SECTION ARE SPECIFICALLY those identified with "entertainment." It is in that area that an image is most likely to become visible. The daily press has not been included and neither has the periodical press—though it might be said to belong at least in part to the entertainment area—since it proved too large and unchartable. It is however not likely that popular periodicals would yield evidence as a whole contradictory to that obtained in the other media.

The methodology aims, as indicated, not only at quantitative results. Since what is ultimately looked for is an *image* with all that the word, as specified, suggests in both totality of impression and significance of details, it was appropriate and even imperative to employ "qualitative," analytic procedures as well. Different media, it was found, require different approaches. In the chapter on books, a systematic description of the contents of every "Jewish novel" published in 1969, for example, would not be likely to give a more authentic view of the Jewish image in books than would the examination of one best-selling novel like *Portnoy's Complaint,* whose hero's name has become a "code" word. Attention was therefore in favor of books in the public eye, and even on the manner of how they are advertised. In the case of the chapter on theatre, a total universe of data within a given period was examined, and more "purely" quantitative results were obtained. In addition, however, typical items were selected for analysis. This was done also in the case of films, although since there are a much larger number of films produced each year than New York plays, it became impossible to produce an *exhaustive* list of relevant films. The time period selected for plays is longer than that selected for films, because of the greater volatility of fashion in films; a shorter period conveys better the *current* film fashion. In the case of TV and specifically the "talk" shows, which seemed most relevant to the present problem, it was not possible to arrange for viewing of all the material on the three simultaneously broadcast evening network shows. Two different schemes of non-biased selection of material were therefore chosen for two separate time periods, each scheme designed to offset the shortcomings of the other (cf. Television chapter). All the relevant data thus obtained were cited and analyzed.

The overall procedure thus consists of both quantitative and "qualitative" methods, a combination dictated by the type of material involved and its various demands on the researcher.

FILMS

AFTER THE "GREAT RETREAT" (CF. INTRODUCTION) IN THE early thirties, the existence of the American Jew was first reacknowledged in American films in the late forties. (At least in a more than incidental manner, such as that of some war films, in which the ethnic spectrum of a military platoon sometimes included the Jewish boy from Brooklyn.) Most importantly, two sensational films appeared at that time, *Crossfire* (1947) and *Gentlemen's Agreement* (1948), both dealing explicitly with anti-Semitism. These were, however, not really films about Jews, but about non-Jews and their involvement with that problem. To wit, the main figure in *Crossfire* is a gentile soldier who kills a Jew (presented fleetingly), and in *Gentlemen's Agreement* it is a gentile reporter who *poses* as a Jew in order to challenge the managements of certain resorts.

A more direct treatment of Jewish characters occurs in *Body and Soul* (1947), about the rise of a boxer from New York's Lower East Side and his subsequent corruption and fall. This film has an Odets-like focus on the natural virtues of the lower classes, in this case the immigrant Jews from which the prize fighter emerges and the abandonment of whose ethos eventually means the destruction of the hero. As in Odets's film *Golden Boy*, the figure of the boxer becomes the symbol of the "good" man of the people destroyed by the machinery of capitalism. But while the good people here are Jewish rather than Italian, as in the Odets film, the film's leftish emphasis is on their social status rather than their religion or ethnicity.

Finally one might mention from this period the two films on Al Jolson, which were mounted in standard show business biography style, meaning sentimental delineation of career and marital ups-and-downs, interspersed with musical numbers. However they also contained the depiction, unusual for this genre, of a father-son relationship that cast a faint shadow of the conflict arising out of the secularization process. The father is a cantor whose feelings about his son's career as a "jazz singer" are not, at the start, entirely positive. The theme is only mildly touched upon, perhaps as a kind of wistful echo of the story of the Al Jolson film *The Jazz Singer* of 1927, which was also the first sound film ever made. In that film the generational conflict between religion and secularism was at the center of the story; the old cantor actually dies from grief at the son's decision in favor of jazz over liturgy. In the later film the father reacts to the son's choice of a jazz career with merely a wan and finally approving smile.

In the fifties, again, there are occasional films whose protagonists are Jewish. Thus, *Marjorie Morningstar*, (1958) based on Herman Wouk's best-selling novel, is the story of a middle-class Jewish girl whose affair with a Jewish showbusiness type leads to disillusion and maturity. In distilling this love story out of the novel, the film loses the book's specifically Jewish locales, its Jewish family milieu, together with the satiric treatment thereof. A more subtle distillation of story from Jewish setting occurs in *Middle of the Night* (1959), one of Paddy Chayevsky's films about Bronx life. The hero is a middle-aged Jewish garment manufacturer in love with his young gentile receptionist. The manufacturer is a widower who lives with his divorced sister, and the domestic scenes, involving also a married daughter and her husband, have all the social verisimilitude to be gained from a reasonably faithful recording of the relevant speech patterns (an attempt somewhat marred by a less than fully convincing reproduction given by Fredric March, the non-Jewish actor who plays the widower). But all sense of history, tradition, values is drained from this family group, as becomes apparent when, in the heated debate as to whether the older man should marry the young girl, nobody even broaches the debating point that, after all, the girl isn't even Jewish. That a conscious reluctance may be at work here about a "full" portrayal of Jews is perhaps borne out by Chayevsky's other films about the Bronx milieu, *Marty, The Catered Affair, The Bachelor Party,* whose main characters tend to be Italian, or Irish, but never Jewish, even though Chayevsky is Jewish and is writing, as must be assumed, out of his own experience.

Films like *Marjorie Morningstar* and *Middle of the Night,* then, convey in their restrained presentation of the American Jew the feeling that they have a timorous sense of audacity about their subject matter. It is interesting in this connection to note that a director whose specialty has been audacity, Billy Wilder, introduces Jewish elements into his films of the forties and fifties, presumably in order to enhance that audacity. In *The Lost Weekend* (1945), a film considered controversial at its appearance because of its detailed depiction of alcoholism, the alcoholic hero is seen at one point wandering on Third Avenue with the intention of hocking his typewriter. But every pawnshop is closed and a man on the street explains that it is Yom Kippur. When the hero asks about the non-Jewish hockshops, the man explains, "We have an agreement. They don't open on Yom Kipper, we don't open on St. Patrick's Day." In *Some Like It Hot* (1959) Wilder dared not only to have his two leading men appear extensively in drag, but to give them Jewish identities. In *The Apartment* (1962) Wilder finally introduces a nearly three-dimensional, though minor Jewish character, the doctor next door, who not only helps rescue Shirley MacLaine after attempted suicide but gives her a dose of the Jewish ethic as summed up in the phrase, "One must be a *mensch*." This last example may reflect the onset of the current period, when it is no longer audacious, really, to refer to the existence of American Jews, but when it apparently still is to do so without being satirical. Wilder's audacity consists here precisely in showing the Jew without satire. In this connection one might mention *The Pawnbroker* (1965), which was indeed a serious film about a New York Jew, but significantly the hero's tragic life in America is depicted as determined totally by his earlier experience in Nazi Europe. The film thus makes a serious statement actually not about the American Jewish but the European Jewish experience.

Turning now to the current film situation, it is possible to find within about two years as many films that have Jewish protagonists as might previously have been found in about a decade. Since the beginning of 1968, for example, one comes across *The Producers, No Way To Treat A Lady, Bye, Bye Braverman, The Odd Couple, I Love*

You, Alice B. Toklas, The Fixer, Goodbye Columbus, The Angel Levine. (This is not an exhaustive list if one considers musicals like *Funny Girl* or *Oliver* as well as many additional comedies of middle-class life with a, possibly, vaguer Jewish touch.) The next thing one notices is that every one of these films is a comedy, except for *The Fixer*. The latter, however, is not about contemporary American Jews at all, but about a turn-of-the-century Russian Jew. It thus appears that while the American Jew is now a possible hero in films, this is only true if he is a *comic* hero.

But what connection, if any, is there between the comic predicaments in these films and a possibly "abnormal" situation of the Jew in American society? Do these comedies reflect directly any of the tensions inherent in what was earlier (in the Methodology chapter) described as ethnic humor?

One of the films, *The Angel Levine*, might qualify. It is about an old, bearded Jewish tailor, played by the comic actor Zero Mostel, whose wife is dying in their Bronx apartment and who is being harassed by a Negro who identifies himself as a Jewish angel. The old tailor is comic as he raises a spoon instead of a knife to threaten the Negro who has invaded his kitchen. But he is shown to be a man tragically bewildered by the fact of America itself: not only the strange black man is an unknown quantity, but the very streets of the Bronx and Harlem he is seen walking. When, in his out-of-style black hat, he asks a policeman for instructions he seems like a new arrival. The comedy as well as the pathos of this film is directly related to the hero's ethnic "conflict" with the American environment.

Now here is a list of the major predicaments occurring in the other films: four Jewish "intellectuals" in exasperated search of a Brooklyn funeral end up at the wrong one (*Bye, Bye Braverman*); two Jewish men sharing an apartment clash like incompatible marriage partners (*The Odd Couple*); a seedy Jewish theatrical producer ineptly schemes with his Jewish accountant to become rich quick (*The Producers*); a Jewish lawyer is drawn into the world of the hippies (*I Love You, Alice B. Toklas*); a Jewish detective is foiled by an eccentric murderer of women (*No Way to Treat a Lady*); a poor Jewish young man courts a Jewish middle-class girl without ultimate success (*Goodbye Columbus*).

These summaries, brief as they are, are probably sufficient to indicate that in none of these films is the humor derived directly from the Jewish–non-Jewish encounter. The Jewish characters shown are in fact very much at home in the American environment. The four men in *Braverman*, being professional critics of the culture, might be expected to be at odds with it. But they display a virtuoso knowledge of comic strip characters that exudes a great at-home-ness, and the only source of momentary annoyance that is distinctly "cultural" arises out of the fact that they are traveling in a Volkswagen. An incident in which the four are stopped by a Negro cab driver looks for some moments as if it might become a minor Jew-Black "confrontation," until it is revealed that the cab driver is himself Jewish. There is actually not a single hint, in any of the above films, of anti-Semitism. On the contrary, there is only a case of anti-gentilism, of a comic kind, generated by the detective's mother (*No Way to Treat a Lady*) who has momentary misgivings about her son's courtship of a non-Jewish girl.

If the comic predicaments, then, are not direct depictions of inter-group conflict, are they the more indirect reflections of such conflict associated with ascribed stereotypical idiosyncrasy? Here a distinction should be kept in mind between idiosyncrasies, meaning peculiar in relation to what is considered the norm, and behavior that makes merely for *diversity* and is really a different way of doing the normative thing. The fact that a rabbi wears a head-covering is not, in this sense, an idiosyncrasy; there is no qualitative distinction per se between a Jewish and a Protestant religious service.

Among the films mentioned, *one* might, in addition to *The Angel Levine,* be said to qualify as a genuine depiction of group idiosyncrasy. In *The Producers* the hero, Max Byalistok (as played by Zero Mostel), is old enough and "foreign" enough to have immigrated from Russia, say, in his teens. His very name hints at this. He is also a theatrical producer, at once insecure and flamboyant. And so he conveys the impression of an uprooted romantic, a marginal man, deprived of one tradition without having found another; a man whose world can only be that of make-believe. This make-believe is true not only of the theatre but of his role as producer, since he is at the end of his tether and sees his salvation only in deliberately producing a flop. But while Bohemian marginality is an idiosyncrasy in which Jews noticeably partake, it is not itself a typical Jewish characteristic, real or ascribed. There is also no explicit reference to Jewishness in the film, unless one is to consider this accomplished by a short soliloquy directed heavenward by the hero that suggests a familiarity with the deity reminiscent of the Patriarchs.

In none of the other remaining films is Jewishness even as much related to comic predicament as it is here. The aspects of Jewishness in these films tend in fact to become more gratuitous in relation to the story the more they are made explicit. In *The Odd Couple,* the least explicit in this respect, it is really the New York-Jewish *temperament* (which could incidentally be put to tragic use as well) that is utilized with good effect in a frenetic comedy situation concerning two divorced men keeping house together. It is a matter of using actors with a certain volatility and urban wryness (Walter Matthau and Jack Lemmon), and dialogue of a certain nervous momentum, to get the most out of a comic predicament itself no more typical of Jews than is tripping over a banana. While Jewishness as a conscious commitment is never alluded to and is as irrelevant for the film as it appears authentically to be for the secularized characters in it, the Jewish *style* is valid, theatrically, for the comic wrangling of the two incompatibles. Two Swedes, given *their* temperament, might have been less funny or, more accurately, funny in a different way. (Cf. Neil Simon, author of *Odd Couple,* on "writing Jewish" in the chapter on Theatre.)

While there is thus an impression in *The Odd Couple* of a kind of valid exploitation of what can only in the broadest sense be considered Jewish idiosyncrasy, the impression of a more gratuitous kind of exploitation is gained in the remaining films. In *Goodbye Columbus,* the comic predicament derives from the upper-middle-class attitude of the girl's family to the less affluent boy, though the young protagonists themselves go through a "straight" (i.e. non-satirical) love story till nearly the very end. The suburban Jewish Mother is given her due as comic figure by being made to say the ritualistic, "Eat, children are starving all over the world," but nothing more in the way of Jewish idiosyncrasy is noticeable in her. If she is meant to be funny, it is by virtue of having been *identified* as Jewish Mother. And then there is a wedding sequence in which a straight shot of a white-capped rabbi (or cantor) officiating at the ceremony, is again, as it were, *proclaimed* funny, without being in itself funny at all. That is, the humorous mood of what precedes this sequence "sets up" the audience so that it laughs, as was witnessed by the writer during a showing, at this shot of the rabbi. This laughter, incidentally, came not because of the comic surprise that a *wedding* is taking place. It is in fact impossible to know just *what* is taking place while only the singing rabbi is shown, but the very next shot is then *intrinsically* funny, showing the awkward bridegroom in ill-fitting top hat. The laughter evoked by this image also proves the audience right in its having assumed the rabbi to be comic. The rest of the wedding sequence then visibly strains to create a *comic* Jewish wedding, perhaps to throw a stronger comic Jewish aura on the rest of the story, since the wedding itself is not central to the plot. There is a preponderance of corpulent females at the buffet table, masticating greedily, and two businessmen guests are pacing the length of the hall to determine the yardage of the carpet.

The humor of the Jewish Mother in *No Way to Treat a Lady* derives again from her middle-class attitude, this time about her son's being a mere cop. She harasses him for his lack of ambition with the standard middle-class chagrin at such a shortcoming. Her comic scene of explicit Jewishness, however, comes when she wonders whether the girl her son is interested in is Jewish. The ironic and casually superior reaction of the girl sets the comic note for the scene. The way the scene is finally resolved, with the mother suddenly totally satisfied because the girl has mumbled something about approving of things Jewish, reveals the totally comic intention behind this encounter. Yet the mother has displayed no idiosyncrasy unless the avowal of her Jewishness and the interest in the identity of the potential daughter-in-law is idiosyncratic. Actually, the comedy of the scene is meant to derive from its explicitness about Jewishness itself.

The story of *I Love You, Alice B. Toklas,* is a farcical one about a middle-aged lawyer forsaking his work, his fiancee, his very clothes, in order to emulate the "lifestyle" of a teen-age hippie girl. Once again, the humor of the situation derives from middle-class attitude (as well as from the hippie attitude it confronts). Once again, there is a Jewish Mother, whose humor, this time not asserted but actually shown, is that of emotional, concerned, but not particularly Jewish, motherhood. (Perhaps the fact that all three of the mothers mentioned are acted by non-Jewish actresses points to the non-concern with "authentic" Jewish idiosyncrasy.) Once again, too, there is Jewish ritual in the form of a wedding ceremony, which turns out to be abortive, incidentally, since the hero escapes before the plighting of the troth. While the situation is a classic comic device, the introduction of Twin Cantors seems again no more than a gratuitous attempt to enhance the comedy by resort to a supposedly funny Jewishness.

In the situation, finally, of the four men driving to a Brooklyn Funeral (*Bye, Bye Braverman*) the comic predicament is that of the reluctance and discomfort of middle-aged, middle-class types in the face of an obligatory excursion to a low-rent neighborhood. As in *Odd Couple,* the "Jewish temperament" is sought in support of the comic effect, and if the results are less successful this may be due to the lesser comic talents of the actors involved. Besides, the two in *Odd Couple* are pitted *against* each other, one being sloppy and devil-may-care, the "man" of the house, and the other fussy and hysterical, the "woman" of the house. This is domestic comedy brought to a higher pitch by the fact that the "woman" is really another guy. And both the exasperation and the prissiness, respectively, are "souped up" by the lively Jewish temperament. In *Braverman,* which is worth a more extensive analysis because it is the most explicitly Jewish of the films mentioned, there is no well-defined conflict like that; the men perched together in the small car merely display slightly different shades of vague melancholy and occasional rancor. The comedy of their predicament is obviously meant to be enhanced not by a real conflict between the characters but by the fact that they are Jews, explicitly designated as such. The result is neither humor *nor* Jewishness. Except for one of the characters, played by Joseph Wiseman, who is an Old Left radical à la Irving Howe (the film is based on Wallace Markfield's *roman à clef, To an Early Grave,* that dealt with the imaginary reaction of some *Partisan Review* types to the death of Isaac Rosenfeld), the characters tend to do and say things that seem based on observation of the comic image Jew. Only the Wiseman character may be said to come close to making an "authentic" Jewish joke, for instance: when the four in the Volkswagen lose their way to the funeral parlor and wander about Brooklyn, he says, "It's not like forty years in the desert, after all. One can ask directions. . . ." He comes close, but a sense of effort on the part of the script-writer clings to the remark, as if he had said, "Now what would be a *real,* old-fashioned Jewish joke at this point?" This sense of bewildered aiming for a quality not really well known pervades the film.

The problem of showing funny Jewish behavior when

there is no conflict to create the humorous tension does not arise in the first part of the film, where each of the characters is shown separately in some form of domestic imbroglio. Here an apparently standard aspect of "arbitrary" Jewish humor is employed: the cliché of the "nincompoop" (cf. Theatre). Thus, when one of the four, George Segal, is awakened in the morning by the phone call from Braverman's wife, who informs him of his friend's death and asks him to come right over, he complains to her that he hasn't had his juice yet. After promising to come and hanging up, his first words to his wife are, "We owed Braverman a hundred and sixty-five dollars!" He proceeds to squabble with his wife, who doesn't want him to go to the funeral. He says he goes to all of *her* family affairs, where he has to meet people he can't *stand*. The wife finally lets him go, but gets even with him: she doesn't make his juice. Segal plays this character with a kind of figurative wink, as if to say, "How Jewish all this is!"

Similar squabbling occurs in the next household. The second character (Jack Warden) is also discovered in bed, before the bad news reaches him; *his* bedmate is Miss Mandelbaum, his mistress. They are fighting because she doesn't want to visit his mother. He says his mother gave her stuffed cabbage and other goodies once. *She* says all she got was hard-boiled eggs. *He* says his mother gave her cartons of stockings; she says his mother gave her "two lousy pair, seconds yet." He says she is so stubborn she didn't even want to stay over in his place after they had been "making it two point six times a week." And so on. That last line of dialogue, surely appropriate in a comedy sketch, most clearly exemplifies the artificiality, familiar though unreal, of these Jewish characters in these supposedly typical Jewish situations. The third character (Sorrell Booke) is discovered fussing before an empty sheet in his typewriter while being distracted by the danger posed to the immaculate body of his Volkswagen outside by playful boys. Only the Wiseman character is not depicted in his first scene as a *schlemiel*, though the sponging son he is shown arguing with unmistakably fits the label.

A comedy sketch device also constitutes the film's climax: the four men are at last in front of the bier upon which is laid what they believe to be the body of Leslie Braverman. Suddenly a strange woman in black rushes up to the corpse and begins shouting, in exaggerated stridency, "Morris! Morris!" But before this denouement—they have come to the wrong funeral—there occurs the film's major comic sequence, the rabbi's funeral oration. That the rabbi is supposed to be funny becomes apparent as soon as the face beneath the skullcap is recognized as that of Alan King, a Jewish Comedian well known from TV. The comedian as rabbi is probably thought of by the devisers of the scene as the peak in comic Jewishness, for when the rabbi, a major staple in the comedian's repertory on TV, actually is embodied in the comedian, the joker and what he jokes about become one, presumably causing a comic explosion. This assumption is indeed apparent in this scene, since its comedy is not drawn from anything approaching "rabbinic humor"—the way, for example, clerical humor is employed by the anti-Catholic Louis Bunuel, or, more benignly, the way the old crotchety priest was played in old Hollywood films by Barry Fitzgerald, an "authentic" Irishman. (Alan King, by contrast, is not of course a Jewish *character* actor.) At the beginning of the scene the illusion is momentarily sustained that the comic aspects of religion are actually going to be explored. The four men have a long ride behind them and they want to see the funeral oration over and done with. The rabbi however seems to be just hitting his stride. "Long playing rabbi," one of the four mutters. But then the speech itself becomes more audible as the camera concentrates on Alan King. It turns out he is not being solemnly religious at all; he is being comically nihilistic. He is giving a comic monologue, in the comedian's typical manner of mock outrage, about how for every good thing in life we also get a bad thing. "Have a little pleasure from the grandchildren? Take a coronary!" He goes on and on with these compensatory pairs, until, ". . . take an enlarged prostate. Let us pray." This is said in one breath, thus achieving, or reaching for, the "topper," the monologue's biggest gag. But this is not milking humor from *characteristic* behavior. It is a depiction rather of the Jewish Comedian's rabbi, encountered in TV and night club monologues. Perhaps the very fact that such a scene does *not* constitute militant anti-religious humor, the rabbi having long ago ceased to be an opponent reflecting the oppressive power of religion, diminishes the need for verisimilitude in the caricature.

Braverman was not a commercial success, but it is nevertheless a compendium of the major techniques of current popular Jewish comedy. One of its minor figures, the Wiseman character, displays some of the characteristics of the idiosyncratic ethnic type also encountered in the hero of *The Producers* and *The Angel Levine*. He is vaguely at odds with the environment, he suggests an Old Testament radical, though his only concrete "protest" concerns riding in a *Volkswagen,* "this legacy from Hitler." More central to the film, and more typical of the current comic Jew in the media, are the other three characters, whose manner of squabbling touchiness does not rest on anything more ethnic than an excessive concern for one's ego, one's comfort, one's possessions. (When his fender is dented, the Sorrell Booke character, owner of the Volkswagen, turns away to shed a quiet tear before attempting to assault the cab driver responsible for the damage.) The comic rabbi, finally, is an extreme case of the *assertedly* funny Jew represented by those three middle-class types. If the Jewish Mother is missing in the flesh, she is at least talked, or more correctly squabbled, about.

The analysis of current films with Jewish protagonists thus shows that while comic, these films most often do not mirror a specifically comic Jew reflecting in turn a specifically comic Jewish situation—i.e., an inter-group situation of tension or conflict. Yet the Jewish group, if judged by the *general* film output, is the only unmistakably comic group, since not only are there no serious films about American Jews, but there is no cumulatively comic presentation of any other group. This is revealed in analysis of film comedy content since the beginning of 1968. Curiously, the funny Irishman, the funny Italian, the funny (though loveable) priest, all formerly known in American films, have become rarities. Altogether, two comedies can be mentioned. One is an Irish comedy, *Quackser Fortune Has a Cousin in the Bronx,* which is however not about an American but a *Dublin* Irishman, and the other is *Lovers and Other Strangers,* whose uncommonness was confirmed by a reviewer who remarked that it "differs in being about the Irish and Italian Catholic rather than the Jewish middle classes" (*The New York Times,* August 13, 1970).

As to Negroes, there have been some comedies, yet,

since these have been outnumbered by serious, "militant" films, it can not be said that there is a cumulatively *comic* Negro film image. What this overall impression actually may come to might be represented by the following juxtaposition of movie ads for films with Negro themes, as found on one particular day in *The New York Times* (August 7, 1970). First ad: "WATERMELON MAN EXPLODES IN LAUGHTER—Show Magazine." Underneath this line, the smiling face of Godfrey Cambridge, Negro comedian; underneath the face, picture of a slice of melon, with stars-and-stripes pattern. Second ad (immediately above foregoing ad): THE MCMASTERS. Underneath this, a picture of a black man and a light-colored woman, groom and bride, captioned "AFTER THE WEDDING—THEY WERE GIVEN A REAL FINE RECEPTION." Underneath this, a picture of enraged white men beating someone. Underneath this, "HE BOUGHT WHITE MAN'S LAND AND A RED MAN'S SQUAW! NO BLACK MAN HAS ENOUGH MONEY TO BUY HIMSELF OUT OF THE TROUBLE HE'S IN NOW!" Third ad (facing the foregoing two on the opposite page): "THEY CALL ME *Mister* TIBBS!" Underneath this, a picture of Sidney Poitier, Negro actor, looking with obvious hostility at the camera; behind this, another picture showing Poitier in the act of giving another man a karate chop.

The overall image of the Negro is thus hardly comic, but even the comedy of *The Watermelon Man* is itself at the expense of the whites rather than the blacks. Its story deals with a white suburbanite whose color inexplicably turns black during one night, and whose comic predicament lies in his frantic need to undo his new Negro identity. He attains dignity finally only after he accepts his blackness, and the last scene shows him training for combat with a group of black militants. Jewish comicality, incidentally, is not overlooked even in this context. At the point in the film when the hero is forced to sell his house in the white suburban neighborhood, the comic climax comes in his remark to his old neighbors who force him to leave: "This neighborhood is too Jewish anyway!"

The possibility of a non-comic depiction of American Jews was demonstrated in the films of the twenties and early thirties. Alongside comedies such as *Potash and Perlmutter,* or *Abie's Irish Rose,* in which the source of the comedy was the heavy baggage of Jewish immigrant idiosyncrasies, there were such tearjerkers as *No Greater Love* (about an old delicatessen owner who, in the words of a review, "sings Hebrew ballads" to the little crippled girl upstairs), *Symphony of Six Million* (about a father who dies at the hands of the son he has struggled to help become a surgeon), *Humoresque* (about the struggles and triumph of a musician), and the above-mentioned *Jazz Singer.* There were also film adaptations of serious plays about Jews, such as Elmer Rice's *Street Scene* (about tenement life) and *Counsellor At Law* (about a brilliant, idealistic Jewish lawyer who is harassed by his wife's Anglo-Saxon family and friends. The reviewer in the *Times* [December 8, 1933] thought the film was "inclined to be anti-Gentile. All of Mr. Rice's admirable characters are Jewish and his disagreeable people are definitely of the so-called Nordic type.") It might be mentioned here, incidentally, that the only "serious" Jewish figure (peripheral) found in the current films examined occurs in *Rosemary's Baby*. It is a doctor called Abraham Saperstein who turns out to be a sinister witch.

To sum up, the Jew, compared to members of other groups, is currently the comic figure *par excellence* in films. At the same time, the comedy of the Jew does not arise out of any indication in the plots or situations of these films that the Jew is today in a *special* position in society that might warrant this comic treatment. It therefore appears necessary to conclude that the Jewish identity is itself a kind of automatic comic device, being projected at an audience "programmed" to receive it. The Jewish Comic Image, in the sense of an arbitrary comicality associated with the Jew and little comedy, of any kind, associated with any other group prevails in the cinema.

THEATRE

THE NEW YORK THEATRE IS THE LEAST "MASS" OF THE MASS media here considered. Yet its importance may not necessarily be reflected in the relative smallness of its audience. Many of the "properties" that first appear on the stage are subsequently turned into films. Moreover, the New York theatre is closely enough aligned with the popular culture to echo prevailing trends of taste and interest, if it does not foreshadow them. This is true of off-Broadway as well as Broadway, especially since the former is now appealing, for economic reasons, to the *total* potential audience.

In surveying the theatre seasons from 1964–1965 to 1969–1970 (cf. Appendix), a problem seems to arise initially in the attempt to ascertain the existence of a Jewish Comic Image. For there is rarely a play (or musical) nowadays without at least a comic component. Even plays not billed as comedy contain large chunks of it, either in the form of comic relief (where the comedy tends to off-set the seriousness) or in the form of "black comedy" (where the comedy tends to reinforce the seriousness). It might thus at first glance seem difficult to isolate a special comic treatment of Jews. *Everything*, more or less, is given some comic treatment. Nevertheless, there *are* serious characters in plays, and there *are* serious problems that are dealt with. And though serious plays and even serious characters may be threaded through with humor, it is still possible to determine whether the Jew is, in a given case, a serious or a comic creation. A simple case in point is Arthur Miller's *The Price* (1967–68 season). Here is a fundamentally serious play, concerning the confrontation of two long-estranged brothers, that contains a large component of comic relief. This relief is furnished in the person of a colorful Jewish octogenarian with Russian-Yiddish accent. Inspection of the script (64) reveals an almost rigid compartmentalization of moods: the Jew has all the laugh-lines, the other characters have all the drama. The striking thing here, incidentally, is that there is internal, as well as external, evidence that the serious characters, the two brothers and the wife of one of them, are also, in conception at least, Jewish characters, but nothing is said about this in the play; the old man's ethnic identity is explicitly referred to, that of the other characters is simply left up in the air. The story itself clearly continues that exploration of the father-and-sons relationship that Miller had begun in *All My Sons* and *Death Of A Salesman*. It was about a Yiddish production of the latter that a reviewer said that it seemed to be the original, of which the English version seemed to be the translation (82). Miller, it was implied, was depicting his Jewish family background.

Concerning *The Price*, where this material is explored further with the father of the earlier play now being dead, and the two sons meeting after a separation of twenty years—one now famous, one obscure—the assumption that autobiography is involved is unavoidable. Indeed, the names of the protagonists, Victor and Walter Franz, and the former's wife, Esther, contain at least the hint that they are not "Anglo-Saxon." (One of the actors engaged to play one of the brothers, though he fell ill before the opening, was Jack Warden, who appeared as one of the characters in *Bye, Bye Braverman*.) Moreover, the brothers in the play reveal that their once-rich father was wiped out in 1929, a fact that also fits Isadore Miller, Arthur Miller's father, a "retired manufacturer who lost much of his fortune in the crash of 1929" (42, p. 209). The language of the characters, again, recalls the language of *Death Of A Salesman*, with its as-if-translated-from-the-Yiddish overtones. In that play, the above-mentioned reviewer noted, the salesman's "repeated claim that his son has failed to find himself 'for spite' becomes more connotative when 'for spite' becomes the Yiddish 'af tsuloches'" (82). And in *The Price*, some of whose language the *Times* critic indeed found "fustian," the reference, for example, to someone sacrificing his life "out of vengeance" seems more natural in the Yiddish "far a nekomeh." This is not necessarily meant to mean (to make one more speculative intrusion into the private life of Arthur Miller) that Yiddish must have been spoken at the Miller home. It merely means that at least the *echo* of the language was there.

The point of this digression concerning the ethnic identity of the serious characters in *The Price* is to suggest that since they were to be *serious*, they could not be avowedly Jewish. The serious Jew, being an incongruity (at least on stage, as will be shown), cannot make a "universal" serious point. Thus even if a Jew is to be a positively drawn hero, as is the old man Solomon in Miller's play, he must be comic. He may be likable, he may be "authentic," he may be wise; but he is not to be taken seriously.

The character of the old man, Gregory Solomon, "nearly

ninety," is typical of the "idiosyncratic" kind of Jewish character in the current theatre. These types do not occur, in any of the plays examined, in connection with a plot of inter-ethnic conflict. In fact, whatever the play's action, they are basically commentators. In this function they are helped by the fact that they are not to be taken seriously: their idiosyncrasies put them beyond the reach of the criticism of other characters. They are thus, in their untouchable wisdom, the expressions of a benign nostalgia for the Jew of the "old school" on the part of certain playwrights, as is the case with Arthur Miller's Mr. Solomon. He is introduced into the play as an old furniture dealer, come to inspect the parental furniture the two brothers have decided to sell. But his dramatic function is to cast the mellow light of his years and his European-Jewish background on the tense setting of recrimination and guilt arising between the brothers. His humor generally has the kind of above-the-scene stance that shows up the inconsequence of social fashion. Yet the first words he utters on entering the play are straight out of the Jewish Comedian's night club. He has just walked up several flights and he is coughing. When asked if he would like a glass of water, he answers "Water I don't need; a little blood I could use" (68 p. 25). This is not the humor of mellow wisdom, but the humor of the Jewish Comedian's *shtik*. Quite unmistakably this entrance serves notice on the audience that here is a funny Jew, so that Solomon's later and less mechanical humor will be received with the proper amusement. Significantly, it seems necessary to Miller to echo the more familiar "inauthentic," i.e. manufactured, humor, before he introduces the authentic but currently less well-known ethnic clown, with old-fashioned accent and point of view.

That homespun point of view, relativistic as to social styles (partially symbolized by the styles of furniture whose ephemeral nature the old dealer points out), but rather fundamentalist as to certain human values, is of course held up in the play for admiration. Compared to the uncertain younger characters, perplexed and anxious about life, Solomon is a Rock of Ages. He tells another character, and the American middle class, what's what:

> What is the key word today? Disposable. The more you can throw it away the more it's beautiful. The car, the furniture, the wife, the children—everything has to be disposable. Because you see the main thing today is shopping. Years ago a person, he was unhappy, didn't know what to do with himself—he'd go to church, start a revolution—*something*. Today you're unhappy? Can't figure it out? What is the salvation? Go shopping. . . . I'm telling you the truth! If they would close the stores for six months in this country there would be from coast to coast a regular massacre. (68, p. 40)

And he makes a plea for the eternal verities:

> Mister, I pity you! What is the matter with you people! . . . Nothing in the world you believe, nothing you respect—how can you live? You think that's such a smart thing? That's so hard what you're doing? Let me give you a piece advice—it's not that you can't believe nothing, that's not so hard—it's that you still got to believe it. *That's* hard. And if you can't do that, my friend—you're a dead man! (68, p. 36)

The author's heart is obviously in these statements, yet the old Jew is nevertheless nearly ninety, his accent and style are droll. If the words carry any conviction, it is *despite* the fact that the character who speaks them cannot be taken seriously. Perhaps the prototype of this wise clown type of Jewish stage character is Tevye, the 19th-century Russian milkman of *Fiddler on the Roof* (1964–65). One reviewer actually says about Mr. Solomon that "he is as Tevye might be after coming to America and making money" (41, p. 12). But the admirability of these characters hinges on their very remoteness from the American scene. If they are not actually foreigners, like Tevye, they are recent immigrants, like the sympathetically comic hero of *The Education of Hyman Kaplan* (1967–68), or they are old-timers, whose attitudes were formed in another era, or in Europe, like Mr. Solomon, or like the old philosopher hero from Coney Island in *The Good Bye People* (1968–69).

By contrast, the Americanized Jew, also a figure of fun in the theatre, is accorded much less sympathy than the "ethnic" Jew. In fact one type of play encountered utilizes comic American Jews as butts of the playwright's hostility, presumably pertaining to both these characters specifically and to the American middle class generally, as whose exemplification the characters are depicted. The comic mode invariably accompanies this hostility. In Arthur Kopit's *The Day the Whores Came Out to Play Tennis* (1964–65), the setting is a Jewish country club on the brink of destruction by some mysterious, unseen prostitutes. The entire action consists of the banter and petty wrangling of some of the club's key members, who make only ineffectual and slightly absent-minded attempts to forestall impending doom. Old Gayne, the club's secretary, is interested only in playing another hand of poker; his son Rudolph (or "Wolf"), the chairman of the sports committee, is a "live wire" making noisy motions of saving the club, but achieving nothing; Herbert, chairman of the junior membership committee, is lengthily involved in the problem of whether Duncan, the butler, has handed him a glass of orange juice, or grapefruit juice, or orange-grapefruit mix, or what. The vulgarity of the exclamation "Schmuck" and of nastily indiscreet stories about the wives is relieved only by the genteelness of objecting that it isn't "nice" to sleep on the bench of the club patio, or that one should treat the butler with maybe a little more consideration. That butler, Duncan, a totally insolent Englishman who claims in mock innocence that he believes his job at the club consists of helping the members of the club with their diction, turns out to be in league with the forces moving in for the attack from outside. He is given a fierce dressing down by Rudolph: "You goddamned son of a bitch! Who gave you the right to make fun of my father's diction! That's the way he *sounds* when he talks. *He can't help it!* . . . I mean what do you *want?* Do you want him to sound like *you* maybe? I mean would *that* make him more acceptable? . . ." (57, p. 130). But when his father thanks Rudolph he also turns on *him:* "You think I did that for *you?* Is that what you think? . . . You stupid *Jew!* . . . I mean you're a joke! You're no *man*" (57, p. 132). The one "noble" speech is thus immediately offset; Rudolph is immediately relieved of all suspicion about harboring sympathetic impulses, just as no such impulses are evident in anyone else. This civilization, with only different degrees of fatuity or vulgarity, appears to deserve its imminent destruction. A lofty symbolism is here unmistakably intended and what is curious is that this universalist tableau is particularized by Jewish characters. "I haven't the faintest idea," George Oppenheimer of *Newsday* wrote in his review, "why the country club is Jewish, except that maybe Mr. Kopit found it easier to make jokes in this atmosphere" (*Newsday,* March 16,

1965). Unless one is to believe that Kopit indeed subscribes to the view of some early socialists, and later of the Nazis, that the Jews are singly responsible for the rise of modern capitalist society, the conjunction of Jews and "civilization" seems arbitrary. There is only the other possibility that use is being made of that audience conditioned to laugh at Jews; it is the humor of the Jewish Comic Image at work.

It should be said that these comedies which, as far as can be ascertained, make more or less savage use of the Jewish caricature are all by Jewish authors, and the vehemence of their attitudes as well as the fact that their targets are middle-aged suggest attack by the Jewish son on the Jewish parent. This motivation also happens to complement very well the requirements of comedy technique utilizing the Jewish Comic Image: with this stone the playwright can kill both the middle-class parent and the laugh-hungry audience. A number of comedies, all in the 1969–70 season, in fact show the son in the actual process of "getting even" with the Jewish father: in *Is That You, Norman?* the son mortifies the father by turning homosexual, in *A Teaspoon Every Two Hours* by bringing home a black girl, and in *The Engagement Baby* by actually being black himself. (In *The Chinese and Dr. Fish* the joke is "switched" and the son mortifies the *Chinese* parents by bringing home a *Jewish* girl.) Yet these are not specifically Jewish mortifications, homosexuals and blacks being "problematic" for American society in general. The Jew himself, supposedly the target of the attack, remains a "front" for the American middle-class ethos.

A third type of play presenting Jewish characters is the "manufactured" comedy, which partially overlaps with the previous category. The designation seems just, since the type seems to aim rather singlemindedly at achieving a maximum productivity of funny moments. Verisimilitude is dispensed with in favor of a comic sketch atmosphere, replete with exaggeration, caricature, and parody. In *Play It Again, Sam* (1968–69), for example, the woebegone hero, just deserted by his wife, attempts to strike up an acquaintance with a girl at an art gallery. When he asks her what she "sees" in the painting she is looking at, she goes into a straight-faced monologue, which is really a parody of pretentious art criticism, to the effect that the painting represents the agony of Man in a meaningless void, Man on the edge of the abyss, and so on. After she finishes, the hero, after a moment's hesitation, asks, "What are you doing Saturday night?" and she answers promptly, without batting an eye, "I'm committing suicide." Thereupon the hero, with the hopeless persistence of the true *shlemiel* of comic fantasy, asks mournfully, "What are you doing *Friday* night?" It is of such artificial "set-ups" that the manufactured comedy is made, and quite frequently the hero, typically a *shlemiel*, is Jewish.

A closer look at these heroes reveals that they are underendowed figures—comically awkward, helpless, bewildered—whose Jewish identity constitutes an additional comic impediment, as if it were, say, a peculiar gait. It is as if the playwright had said, "Let's make him funnier by saying (or suggesting) he's Jewish." Though this hero typically is younger than either the ethnic or the parent type, his grotesqueness does not permit the conclusion that the Jewish playwright is really writing about himself. The Life of the Author as a Young Jew is not a genre found in the theatre.

Since the type of play in which this *shemiel* hero turns up tends to chalk up the longest runs, it can be said that this comically woebegone hero is the most typical Jew on the American stage. In play after play he is served up via the same recipe: place hero into a commonplace predicament and watch him wriggle for two acts. What actually renders the predicament commonplace is the way the hero reacts to it: helplessly, hysterically, above all, without dignity. The *shlemiel's* status is established at once by showing how, when stricken, he immediately starts to make every motion appropriate to a futile outcome. He wrestles unsuccessfully with inanimate objects, is unable to organize any sensible movement of his own extremities, and encounters people as if they were speeding automobiles.

As to the nature of the predicament itself, three of the plays examined present the identical one: the absconded wife. (*The Odd Couple* [1964–65], *Scuba Duba* [1967–68], *Play it Again, Sam* [1968–69]). A fourth play, *Something Different* (1967–68), had a rather similar predicament: a playwright's absconded muse. This play has a more explicit Jewish aspect than the others. The hero, a "blocked" writer, is possessed by the notion that only by re-creation of all the circumstances surrounding an earlier burst of creativity, including the presence of an immigrant-type Jewish Mother, can he write again. Therefore, among other efforts, he requests an employment agency to send him someone to impersonate his mother and ends up interviewing a number of unlikely applicants, including a buxom Negress who speaks fluent Yiddish. This tongue, incidentally, has itself a potent comic image in the theatre. "*Everything*," says Goldman of a Buddy Hackett–Eddie Fisher Appearance at the Palace, "*everything* spoken in Yiddish gets a laugh" (32, P. 13). The way not infrequently chosen to boost even this sure-fire laugh-provoker is to have it spoken by a Negro.

But returning to the predicament of the departed wife, its frequent use seems justified by its appropriateness to the essential *shlemiel*. In each of the three plays mentioned, the wife is already gone by the time the curtain rises, and the first glimpse of the hero shows him on his back, as it were, hopelessly writhing. Immediately the point is made that without his wife the hero is not a man but a lost infant. On this note of incongruity, the spectacle of a character who *looks* like a man acting like a child, rests the comedy of the entire play. The Jewishness, thrown in to enhance the comedy, is generally hinted at, rather than stated. *Play it Again, Sam,* for instance, is perhaps Jewish only in that its author, Woody Allen, wrote it as a "vehicle" for himself. Allen is identified in his public persona as a Jewish Comedian, and he carries this persona into the play. That the character is nevertheless established as Jewish, even when actors other than Woody Allen play the hero, can be seen from a capsule description of the play in *The New Yorker:* "Bob Denver as a sort of young Jewish Lear, or maybe Othello—anyhow, not Romeo" (February 28, 1970).

Scuba Duba is Jewish by virtue of references to Queens and such locutions as the distraught hero's opening remark, on hearing loud music coming through the window of the French villa whence his wife has fled: "I really needed this. This is exactly what I came here for" (26, p. 9). The sound is New York Jewish, deriving from Yiddish speech patterns, and it is this matter of speech that also constitutes the Jewishness of *The Odd Couple,* whose suddenly wifeless hero becomes the fussy, dust-hating "wife" of a sloppy, easy-going pal. Neil Simon, its author, distinguishing between "writing Jewish" (*Odd Couple*) and "writing gentile" (*Barefoot in the Park*) says that "the phraseology is different." But he also says that "Jewish is martyrdom, and self-pity and 'everything terrible happens to me'" (32, p. 148). It might not be unreasonable to suggest that Simon has in mind here not so much "Jewish" as "Jewish Comic Image," as encountered in other plays.

Certainly "martyrdom, self-pity, and 'everything happens to me'" is the note struck by the hero throughout Bruce Jay Friedman's *Scuba Duba*. His wife has run away, supposedly with a Negro skindiver. He is alone in the French villa where he has come with his wife for a vacation, and there commences a long parade of impositions and annoyances, piling up on the hero's already heavily burdened head. The initial disturbing music is followed by a bikini-clad nymph, a celebrity-hungry French landlady, an American tourist bully, a French burglar, a French gendarme bully, the hero's mother, long-distance, the hero's psychiatrist bully, the psychiatrist's brassy girl friend, the self-righteous wife herself, a jive-talking Negro bully, and finally the wife's super-dignified Negro lover. In the face of this string of assaults, Harold, the hero, displays such mannerisms as shouting threats out the window, provided he knows there is no one out there; repeatedly cutting the air with a scythe; crying quietly; displaying frantic attachment to a muffler he has had since he was ten; covering himself with clothes and blankets when speaking on the phone, "for privacy." But he is nevertheless not an individual, but rather he *consists* of these not unfamiliar cliché mannerisms of the *shlemiel,* just as every other character in the play comes equipped with *his* appropriate cliché mannerisms. The successive encounters between Harold and these characters are really comedy sketches, consisting of the comic clash between contrasted mannerisms. The American tourist, for instance, is farcically bigoted. He pronounces that the French literally stink; he inquires if there's "a chink's" nearby, and when told there is a Vietnamese restaurant, he says, "As long as they got those egg rolls I don't care what kind of chink they are" (26, p. 23). He is also convinced that in China there are four-year-old prostitutes: "Girl gets to be eight and she's still got her cherry, old Mao Tse-Tung gives her a goddamned peace prize" (*ibid.*, p. 24). The French gendarme consists only of his anti-American *ressentiment*. When Harold sincerely congratulates him on catching the burglar roaming the villa, the gendarme says, "Just because you Americans have everything and we have nothing does not mean you can make fun of me" (*ibid.*, p. 76). Later, the Negro frogman in full regalia has a heavy "Negro style" (shown to be used by him ironically), while the Negro who is the wife's lover affects an exaggeratedly "respectable" language. When Harold shouts at the latter for seducing his wife, the frogman taunts him with, "He ain't gonna be one of them mature adults. He gonna fetch the debbil on that poor old colored man. He gonna reach around there and work some roots. Whoooooooeeeeee"(*ibid.*, p. 114). The seducer himself, however, is all elegance: "Mr. Wonder (Harold), I've had my fill of this vulgar exhibition . . ." (*ibid.*, p. 153).

These characters, then, are all cardboard cutouts. In fact the mother, calling long-distance from Queens, is seen in a *literal* cardboard cutout, while Harold talks to her over the phone. Finally, an obvious touch of nonrealism at the end of the first act: Harold is sitting with the girl in the bikini and talking about his wife. "She'll be here in twenty minutes flat. Have I steered you wrong once tonight?" There follow the ensuing stage instructions: "(Both watch curtain come down.) Curtain" (*ibid.*, p. 71).

Scuba Duba is thus not a realistic account of one man's particular experience. It is rather a display of caricatures. Yet there is a crucial difference between the hero and the characters he plays against: the brutal crassness of the American tourist, the touchy anti-Americanism of the Frenchman, the weird exoticism of the Negro are obviously meant to be taken tongue-in-cheek, by virtue of the very exaggeration of their traits, but the Jewish hero's impotence and frenzy are drawn close enough to nature to enable an audience to identify with this victim facing those monsters. And so the feeling arises about this protagonist that while he is not within a realistic play portraying realistic characters, he is himself nevertheless nearly real. That is, he may be a type, but somehow believable. Thus it becomes possible for the audience to come away from this play not for a moment believing that it has seen a real Frenchman, or Negro, yet fully believing that it has seen a real, and at the same time typical, Jew.

One way Harold seems more real than his antagonists is that, despite being a whining infant, he also seems somehow "reasonable." When he threatens his wife, who has returned for a few "things," with a temper tantrum, he sounds reasonable: "Jennie, what do you want to see, a stretcher case? A French nervous breakdown? You're going to get one, you know. I'm going to sail into one any second now" (*ibid.*, p. 118). He gives fair warning. When he frenziedly knocks the taunting Negro down, he then says, "Jesus, what the hell did I do? . . . Look, I'm really sorry. I just realized what happened. Will you accept my apologies? . . ." (*ibid.*, p. 152). But this touch of reasonability not only makes it possible for the audience to recognize itself—especially in its mellow mood while watching the play—it is also part of the very impotence of the character depicted. He may shout bloody murder to himself when alone in a room, but he is mainly apologetic when facing his antagonists. Thus, as the wife leaves at last, accompanied by the two Negroes, Harold can only shout, after everyone has gone, that he'll throw his wife "right out of the goddamned house" (*ibid.*, p. 158), thus having his futile last word. The viewer both sympathetically identifies with him and yet laughs, secure in the knowledge that surely *he* would never act that way, should such a situation arise. This is, of course, the age-old reaction to the classic "patsy," and the key to the popularity of that figure in comedy. It is this figure, however, that the comic Jew is strongly associated with in the current entertainment media. This figure, as has been suggested, is to the audience a hint of "what I *might* be, but thank God am not." It is what the other guy is. Under the circumstances, the other guy is the Jew.

So far in this chapter, three types of comic stage Jew—the "foreigner," the parent, and the *shlemiel*—have been distinguished. These three are indeed the main types, and others encountered are combinations or variations of them. Altogether, of the plays between the seasons 1964–65 and 1969–70, 46 were found to have Jewish characters. Only five of these plays (*Sign in Sidney Brustein's Window* [1964–65], *The Other Man* [1967–68], *Cabaret* [1966–67], *The Penny Wars* [1969–70], *Inquest*, [1969–70]) had Jewish characters that were not comic. Moreover, three of these five (*Other Man, Cabaret, Penny Wars*) deal with non-American Jews. The "serious" American Jew is indeed a rarity on the American stage. Nor is the comedy of the American Jew based on the problem of minority conflict with the majority culture. Even the "ethnic" types contend with "modernity" rather than with the gentile majority.

The Jew is thus overwhelmingly a comic creature in the theatre, often less than benignly conceived, and more importantly, an "arbitrary" comic creature for the most part (cf. On Method). There is of course an old tradition of the comic stage Jew in America, going back to the vaudeville stage of the late 19th century and beyond. As for unsympathetic Jews, they were the only kind seen in the American drama of the late 18th and all through the 19th centuries. According to a study of Jews in the American drama, these plays, unlike the great majority of plays about Jews today, were by gentile playwrights, since Jewish American playwrights of the 19th century had "no Jewish characters in their plays. . . . To present him (the Jew) as a villain would have meant self-stultification, and to picture him as a decent and human character would have been in defiance of the centuries-old tradition that in the drama the Jew must be the villain, or the subject of derision" (67, p. 7).

Judging by today's theatre, that tradition seems not to have died out. The comic Jew, if not always the villain, has indeed become an *important* Broadway commodity at least since the smash hit *Potash and Perlmutter* of 1913, which concerned two wrangling business partners whose hearts of gold came into view whenever serious crisis loomed. Yet there was also a period when Broadway presented *serious* characters who were sympathetic Jews. The study mentioned above cites a large crowd of these. They include a soldier from Chicago stationed in Cuba, 1900, who refers to his pride in his "Jewish blood" and risks his life in an experiment to test the cause of yellow fever (Sidney Howard *Yellow Jack*, 1934); the idealistic son of a struggling Bronx family, who decides in the last act to devote his life to the improvement of society (Clifford Odets *Awake And Sing*, 1935); a young radical who fearlessly attacks, in public, company unions, big business, wars (John Howard Lawson *Marching Song*, 1937); a plucky young lawyer, rising from the ghetto to a brilliant and idealistic practice (Elmer Rice *Counsellor At Law*, 1931); another attorney, defending the nine Scottsboro Negroes, crusading for justice (John Wexley *They Shall Not Die*, 1932); an old man who quotes from Bible and Talmud and lives by what he preaches (Maxwell Anderson *Winterset*, 1935); a college instructor discharged from the university because he has led a protest march against a senator (Elmer Rice *We, The People*, 1932); a physician dropped from a hospital, first victim of a retrenchment drive, who arraigns the "rich gentiles" in society for being callous about human rights (Clifford Odets *Waiting For Lefty*, 1934); finally, a number of Jewish mothers, of the type that owns a small shop, or pushcart, and "works day and night for the advancement of her children."

Like the Jewish-American novel of the thirties, the theatre of that decade did not always perceive the immigrant generation as comically quaint, but could convey some of the passion and pathos of that generation's experience. Thus, the grandfather of the young idealist in *Awake and Sing* is a man who has attached high hopes to his new life in America. The shattering of those hopes is suggested when the impatient daughter plucks the father's favorite Caruso record off the phonograph and smashes it.

Of the younger serious characters, many are radicals and thus mouthpieces of their authors' points of view, reflecting the depression and the Jewish involvement in that era's volatile left-wing activity. To some extent, therefore, the seriousness of these Jewish characters must be ascribed to the plays' prevailing tone of agitation; the presentation of *serious* Jews on stage may itself be interpreted as an expression of revolutionary defiance. As a matter of fact, even the grandfather of *Awake and Sing* fits this interpretation: in addition to loving the voice of Caruso, he is depicted as reading avidly in the works of Marx. It might be noted that the most *Jewish* Jew in the above list is probably the character in *Winterset* who is the creation of Maxwell Anderson, the only non-Jewish playwright mentioned.

Currently young Jews, or young men of "Jewish background," are again prominent in radical activity, but among the plays of the last six seasons just one serious Jewish character of that kind was noted (*Sign in Sidney Brustein's Window* [1964], by the non-Jewish Lorraine Hansberry). To be sure, the current radicalism displays a style whose elements, bohemian and "dionysiac," tend to make Jewish identity, as any other identity, irrelevant. Besides, in the thirties Jews could still be counted among the "oppressed." But generally "messages" are transmitted from the stage currently not via impassioned speeches but via rock music and pop humor. One could imagine the theatre of the thirties snapping up a theme like the martyrdom of Goodman and Schwerner; yet the only play in the last five seasons about the Jewish response to black aspirations is a bizarre comedy, *Carry Me Back to Morningside Heights* (1968), in which a young Jew, absurdly guilt-ridden, forces his services as bona fide slave on a reluctant Negro, with the resultant opportunities for facile turn-about humor.

It still remains to be seen whether, and to what extent, other minorities are treated humorously. Firstly, there were in the same time period an undetermined number of plays about Negroes; these were invariably "message" oriented and thus serious in intent. As to plays with minority-group characters other than Jews or Negroes, only twelve were located in the six-year period (cf. Appendix). These, except for one about a Puerto Rican, deal with the Irish or Italians, with or without Catholic emphasis, and eight of them have serious themes and their leading minority-group characters are seriously depicted. (*Matty, the Moron, and the Madonna* (1964–65), *Hogan's Goat* (1965–66), *Not a Way of Life* (1966–67), *That Summer, That Fall* (1966–67), *A Whistle in the Dark* (1969–70), *Borstal Boy* (1969–70), *Cry For Us All* (1969–70), *Child's Play* (1969–70). The comic heroes of three of the remaining four plays (*I Was Dancing* (1964–65), *Minor Miracle* (1964–65), *Mike Downstairs* (1967–68) are Italians or Irishmen of the "ethnic philosopher" type; one is a priest (*Minor Miracle*). They are unequivocally "admirable" characters, with a high quota of seriousness and pathos. It might be added that in two of these three plays (*I Was Dancing, Minor Miracle*) a comic Jew, with Yiddish accent, is introduced in each instance as friend of the hero. It must be assumed that the function of these Jewish figures is to heighten the comedy, since these "friends" have no more intrinsic purpose than the delivery of set monologues or comic *shtiks*. As to the Puerto Rican hero of the fourth comedy (*Steam Bath*, 1969–70), he is a kind of comic God disguised as steam bath attendant who was described by one critic as speaking strangely Jewish lines (cf. Appendix).

This invasion by Jewish comic types (or lines) of plays

about the members of other groups might be taken as an index of how complete is the identification of the Jew with comedy in the theatre. But the comparative tallies make this very clear. During six New York seasons there were 41 plays offering comic Jews (or 43, if the subsidiary comic Jews of the Irish plays are added), and there were four plays presenting comic non-Jewish "ethnics" (excluding Negro characters). On the other hand, there were only two plays showing "serious" American Jews as against eight showing serious Irish and Italians.

It can be said in conclusion that in view of the special identification of the Jew with comedy and the importance in this connection of a kind of arbitrary, gratuitous humor (unrelated by interior evidence to the Jewish situation in America), a Jewish Comic Image exists in the theatre.

TELEVISION

TO CONVEY AN IDEA OF THE "TREATMENT" OF SEPARATE groups on television, it has seemed best to concentrate on the evening "talk" shows, where reasonably spontaneous remarks, uttered by a large variety of spokesmen, as well as the spontaneous or prepared remarks of the country's comedians, are most likely to be heard. In combining "performance," in the form of prepared comic monologues, with conversation on diverse topics, the talk shows—unlike the evening variety shows, which are scripted—transmit back to the public, through what is said and even through how the studio audience responds, a reasonably direct mirror image of the public's own attitudes; these in turn are of course a partial reflection of what the media send out. As to the regularly scheduled "series" that make up most of the remaining evening programming, they do not generally risk the controversial and their treatment of sub-cultures might be said to be informed by the desire to prove that everybody is really "human." *The Flying Nun* series, for example, showed that nuns have a sense of humor and the *Bill Cosby Show* demonstrates that blacks have everyday experiences and emotions. The two comic leading characters in *The Odd Couple,* though their group identity is not specified, are the Jewish representatives of this genre.

The method chosen for assessment of the talk shows pertaining to the image they convey of the Jew and, in comparison, of other ethnic and/or religious groups, is to quote herein all relevant statements, serious or comic, heard within two separate periods, followed in each case by a content analysis.

Since three of the talk shows are broadcast simultaneously each evening, the ideal procedure here would of course have been to arrange for the monitoring of the three shows on three sets by three viewers. This was however not possible and so two alternate procedures, a different one for each of the two time periods covered, were used. The following procedure applies to the first time period:

Of the four talk shows viewed each evening, one (The David Frost Show) was seen *in toto,* since it is broadcast earlier than the other three. For the three simultaneously broadcast shows, the newspaper listings were consulted in advance. In these listings appear the names of the "guests" for a given evening, and so it was possible to attempt listening at least to all or most of the comedians announced for a particular day. (Comedians because it is the *comic* group image that is of interest.)

Where two comedians were appearing at the same time on two channels, an effort was made to hear parts of both appearances. Where, at a given point of time during an evening, no comedian was being seen on any of the three channels, the first interview encountered (with a guest other than a comedian) was recorded. Thus it was possible to obtain a random sample of *serious* occasions as well. Most importantly, bias was avoided in the selection process in favor of one comedian over another, or in favor of one interview over another.

Where there are gaps of several days between quotes, this may be due either to non-appearance of relevant statements, or to non-scheduling of shows due to weekends or holidays. It should be borne in mind that citations are often shortened versions of the original remarks, but deletions in no case affect the meaning of the remarks. Furthermore, when one particular person told a great number of consecutive jokes of identical significance for this study (e.g. Myron Cohen, November 17, 1969), only one or two of the jokes were cited. The quoting of *all* jokes, or remarks, produced in a row by one man seemed unnecessary since the actual number of separate "occasions" rather than the number of jokes is what determines the final quantitative determination. This procedure avoids the possibility of obtaining a (misleading) result showing that, say, Greeks have a strong comic image simply because one man on one show happened to give a monologue consisting of a long string of jokes concerning Greeks.

Below, then, are the statements heard on four talk shows—David Frost, Merv Griffin, Tonight, Joey Bishop—pertaining to ethnic and/or religious groups over the period October 30–November 29, 1969. The remarks relating to Jews are listed first, followed by a listing of the remarks concerning other groups.

October 30, 1969 Joey Bishop Show
Tony Martin (in response to Bishop's mock complaint about Martin's subdued singing style): I'm *dovening* (Yiddish for praying).

November 6, 1969 David Frost Show
George Jessel: ... And then the Arab told the genie his third wish. He said "Destroy the Hebrews." Immediately all the other gifts he had received disappeared. It was a Jewish genie!

November 6, 1969 Merv Griffin Show
Shecky Greene: They called me down before the Committee to testify (about gambling) ... The chairman asked me my name and I said "Shecky Greene." He asked me, "Is that your real name?" and I said, "No, it's Shmuel Greenfield," and he said, "All right, don vorry, I'm just gonna esk you a couple questions." He asked me, "What do you know about 'skimming?' " I said, "I know my mother used to do it to chicken soup." Now my mother's in Leavenworth ...
There was this long line waiting for tables and in front stood this guy who said his name is Peterson and that he had a reservation. The waiter said, (French accent) "There is no Mr. Peterson on my list." Mr. Peterson handed him a fifty-dollar bill and the headwaiter said, "Ah, yes, Mr. Peterson, right on top here." Suddenly a voice from the back says, (Yiddish accent) "I'm Mr. Peterson's friend." The waiter said, "But Mr. Peterson did not mention a friend." The guy from the back comes forward and slips him a hundred-dollar bill. "Oh," says the headwaiter, "*you* are Mr. Peterson." ...
Chill Wills (Western actor, tells of drinking with Greene): Well, there lay a kosher New York boy under the table ...
Richard Dawson (does funny bird calls): ... Part of this call can only be heard by Jewish Airedales. Tonight

a Jewish Airedale will raise his head and say, "Vat's dis?"...
(He mentions "Rashnapur" and is asked what it is) It's Yiddish for "Oy Vey."

November 7, 1969   David Frost Show
Mark Russell: Then there was the Republican Convention. Never have there been so many gentiles in Miami Beach at one time.

November 7, 1969   Merv Griffin Show
Jack Carter: I have that half-Jewish, half-Italian car: a Mazzerata . . . (After someone says there are six people present and they could form a sextet): Let's get four more and we'll have a *minjan* (Jewish prayer quorum) . . .
(After some French conversation between two others, to audience): *Sei hob'n gesogt* . . . ("They were saying . . ." in Yiddish) . . .
B. S. Pully: I can't tell you how much money I won gambling because I owe two people money: gentiles and Jews.

November 8, 1969   Tonight Show
Carson: How can people have such opposed views about the same book (*Portnoy's Complaint*)?
Truman Capote: That depends on whether you're a friend of Philip Roth's or not. . . . I mean there is a Jewish literary Mafia in New York that extends from Columbia University all the way down to the Little Magazines. . . . They tend to push each other's work . . .
Carson (to *Photoplay* reporter): What did they do after the (Academy Awards) ball?

Photoplay Reporter: They said *Kaddish*. You know what *Kaddish* means.
Carson: Sure. It's the Jewish prayer for the dead. You're not talking to a meatball, you know.

November 10, 1969   Tonight Show
David Steinberg (after having done parody of Jezebel): When I do Moses or Jezebel I usually get letters from Reform rabbis. They ask me, "Who *are* these people?" . . .
Bill Dana: . . . And so I was *shwitsing* around . . . You know what *shwitsing* means . . . (Audience gives this a big laugh)

November 10, 1969   Merv Griffin Show
Shelley Berman: Alice Toklas, you know, the woman who put marijuana in Halevah (Yiddish pronunciation of Halvah) . . .
(Does hangover routine) What *is* my name, anyway. Oh yes, it's Sam. Sam what? Wait a minute, let me think . . . It's Spero . . . or Spiro? . . .

November 12, 1969   Merv Griffin Show
Sam Levenson: They get married so young. I went to that wedding the other day, the rabbi said to the groom, "Repeat after me: 'With all my worldly goods I thee endow' . . ." I heard the father whisper, "There goes his bicycle."

November 12, 1969   Joey Bishop Show
Jan Murray: Frank Sinatra? He's my rabbi . . .

November 13, 1969   Tonight Show

Carl Reiner (to Peter Lawford, who has removed his shirt, and his tie, and still wears a pendant around his neck): How about the *Mezuzah?* (Jewish religious object attached to door posts, or worn on necklace.)

November 15, 1969 Tonight Show

Dick Shawn: They're going to have a special Christmas show for the kiddies in Las Vegas: a Santa Claus in the nude. They'll call it "Nude Nick." (Yiddish for "pest") . . .

Betty Walker, does long comic routine as "Martha Tuperman" gossiping on the telephone with her friend "Ceil."

November 17, 1969 Merv Griffin Show

Myron Cohen (uses Yiddish accent to tell jokes): Two men are sitting in Miami Beach and one says to the other, "Let them go to the moon. We are gonna get a capsule and go to the sun. There we'll look for property, you know, super markets." "But we'll burn to death." "Don't be silly. We'll go at night."

Griffin (to Cohen): Is it all right for a gentile to tell a Jewish joke?

Cohen: If it's done with intelligence and good taste.

Griffin: Well, I once told this to a synagogue group who had invited me, and there was like eight seconds of silence after I finished. Then they laughed.

Cohen: That's because they didn't *expect* it from you . . .

Griffin: The story was about these nuns being pronounced the brides of God as they enter the order. They're having this kind of marriage ceremony and the bishop notices some men there. There are not supposed to be any men present. So he asks them, "Pardon me, but may I ask what you are doing here?" and they answer, "We are rabbis. Relatives of the groom."

November 19, 1969 Joey Bishop Show
Sammy Davis (singing *I've Got You Under My Skin*): "Don't you know, little Shmool, you never can win" ("Shmool" is the Hebrew for "Samuel")

November 21, 1969 Joey Bishop Show
Joey Bishop (in mock argument with his gentile announcer): ... And where does it say the Jewish kid has to carry the Christian kid for the rest of his life?

November 25, 1969 Tonight Show
George Burns: Jack Benny wanted to surprise me, so he stood on his bed naked, with a glass of water on his head. I sent in the maid instead. So there he stood, this old Jew, naked ...

November 29, 1969 Tonight Show
Shecky Greene: ... Instead of telling night club audiences I'm Jewish I say if I was with Moses at the Red Sea I'd have made the trip. Moses would have said, "You gotta go. I took out a page in the Bible for it." ... You know, Sammy [Davis] revolutionized our Temple. We used to go ... (sings a very "oriental" melody). Now we go ... (sings words of a Hebrew prayer, "Boruch atto," with a jazz beat).

The following list contains all the remarks heard during the same period concerning groups other than Jews.

October 31, 1969 Merv Griffin Show

Danny Thomas: I find the only benefits I'm giving are for Catholics and for Jews. The Jews with their hospital drives, and the Catholics with their Bingo parties. You know, some of these raffles are fakes. If the parish is very poor, the turkey wins. . . . I only go to Jewish and Catholic affairs. I can't find any poor Protestants.

November 1, 1969   Tonight Show
Slappy White (black comedian): I was there (at the Onassis wedding). One of *us* has to be everywhere these days. . . . Duke Ellington has so much rhythm, they made him an honorary Catholic.

November 5, 1969   Tonight Show
Bill Cosby (black comedian): "Miracle White?" I'd never buy that!

November 6, 1969   David Frost Show
George Jessel: A New England minister told his bishop that he had been away for a few weeks and when asked where he had been said, "In the arms of another man's woman—my mother." The bishop was highly amused and was eager to tell the same story. At the earliest opportunity he told another bishop, "I've been away, you know." When asked where he was, he answered, "In the arms of Reverend Smith's mother."

November 6, 1969   Merv Griffin Show
Nipsy Russell (black comedian): I'm not going to talk about Howard Hughes. He's liable to send me back to Africa, and I'm not liable to turn in my Cadillac for an elephant.

November 8, 1969 Tonight Show

Johnny Carson (as "Karnak," who gives questions to answers):
Answer: Second to none.
Question: Whom would you call for a duel with a Mother Superior?

November 11, 1969 Merv Griffin Show

Merv Griffin (to Rocky Graziano): . . . What about Dean Martin? Don't you like him? He's Italian, like you.
Graziano: Oh yeah. I'm crazy about Italians. . . . Listen, I like Italians, Jews, Negroes, Chinese. This country's been great to me.

November 13, 1969 Tonight Show

Kaye Ballard: This building doesn't look very secure to me. If anything should give way, you'll see one crushed Italian here . . .

November 18, 1969 Merv Griffin Show

Bishop Fulton Sheen: Milton Berle said he saw me driving up in a Rolls Royce with stained glass windows . . . An old pastor wanted to raffle off his old gray mare. The mare died. So he said we'll hold another raffle to find out who lost . . . I wanted to give away a church in Rochester, to start a trend in other cities, so as to make possible new housing in the inner cities. . . . My plan failed. . . . Ever since we split the atom, the world has been split. The generations have been split, the churches have been split . . .
Griffin: Is it the Episcopalians who caused that? . . .
Sheen: . . . Pope John was visiting a prison and he came across a man who had killed his wife. John said to

him, "You know, I was never married, but if I had been I might have killed my wife too..."

November 26, 1969 Tonight Show
Joe Garagiola: When the Pope took away St. Christopher, I think he gave him to the Mets...
Pat Henry (telling of early night club performances): The manager made signs from the kitchen (makes threatening gestures). I think they were Italian...

A look at the yield, on the preceding pages, of four weeks of unbiased viewing of talk shows (except for the bias in favor of comedy) reveals that there were 23 comic Jewish "occasions" against 11 for all other groups combined. Of these, the Catholics, with four, had the highest score. But not only a quantitative distinction is possible; there are important qualitative distinctions as well. The especially easy laughter by the audience actually observed in response to the humor concerning Jews bears witness to the familiarity of that humor, and a somewhat rigorous analysis seems in order for the purpose of uncovering the layers of implied meaning beneath this crust of familiarity and ready response.

The first of the items listed (October 30) might be taken as a start. The situation is as follows: Tony Martin, professional popular singer, is being given a mock lesson in singing by the non-singing Joey Bishop. Bishop asks Martin to try to sing a phrase in a louder, more spectacular way, and Martin thereupon deliberately sings in a muffled, mumbling sort of way instead. When Bishop shows amazement at this decline instead of the hoped-for improvement, Martin says, maintaining the humorous atmosphere, that he is "dovening"—i.e. saying a Jewish prayer. In relation to the probably very small part of the audience in the studio that comprehends the remark, the laughter is louder than might be expected. But putting aside for the moment the phenomenon of laughter at incomprehensible Yiddish expressions, what does this "inside" joke convey to the initiated? This is worth exploring, for this joke is an example belonging in what might be called the religious category of funny remarks concerning Jews on TV. What happens in this instance is that Martin has deliberately done a bad job of singing, for comic effect; he then "justifies" his inadequate performance by calling it "dovening." The inferior behavior, in other words, is appropriate for dovening, but not for singing. Dovening, then, must be an inferior activity. The humor is of course first of all due to the deliberately poor job of singing, but the use of "dovening," tacitly understood, at least among "insiders," as a way of comic evaluation, sets the comic seal on the bad performance.

Exploration reveals another layer of inside humor. Tony Martin, the popular singer with the name that sounds as if it is Americanized Italian, is for a moment forgetting, seemingly, to keep up his public front and is revealing a back-stage "secret" about himself—he is "only" a Jewish boy, for whom dovening comes as naturally, or more naturally than, elaborate singing. But he is of course at the same time signalling with his eyes that he is only kidding, and that he is really not at all likely to lapse into dovening. So, Tony Martin ends up being Tony Martin after all, in fact a Martin displaying that he is *secure* enough to pretend for a moment that he is something "less" than Martin. What is significant here is that casually implicit in that short remark is a definite point about a Jewish religious practice. It is that the practice is somehow shabby and certainly unworthy of a man whose standing with the public is as high as Tony Martin's presumably is.

A similar attitude is implicit in the other instances where there is reference to aspects of Jewish religious practice. In every case the religious expression used becomes a mock description of something to be deprecated, and in every case the humor also is partially due to that element of pretended "self-revelation." Thus, when Jack Carter, Jewish Comedian, responds to the suggestion that the six people present form a sextet by saying (Nov. 7) that they should get "four more and we'll have a *minyan*" (prayer quorum), he is making fun of the group present (or the entire idea of *forming* groups) by means of the word *minyan,* thus alluding to an absurdity inherent in that word and the practice it describes, as well as comically shaking the audience, or at least the "insiders," by revealing openly that he is really "just" a man familiar with *minyans* but awkward about sextets. Again, in the case of the *Photoplay* reporter (Nov. 8), the crestfallen atmosphere at the Academy Awards ball after the unsuccessful presentation ceremony is caricatured by use of the word *kaddish* (Jewish prayer for the dead), and, once more, in the case of Carl Reiner (Nov. 13), the pendant around the neck of Peter Lawford, who has just stripped to the waist, is lightly mocked as a *mezuzah* (Jewish religious object). In every case, the way the particular word is used implies a negative evaluation of what the word actually denotes. One only has to substitute in the imagination equivalent religious expressions of, say, the Catholics (crucifix, saying Mass, and so on) in the casual contexts outlined above to perceive the implications expounded.

As has been suggested, the religious category in Jewish

humor is an insiders' category, since the expressions used are in the main esoteric and likely to be known by few others besides those with more or less intensive Jewish upbringing. But this inside quality points quite unmistakably back to the intramural ironies of the European Jewish emancipation period (cf. Humor of Emancipation, Humor of Non-Emancipation) when such joking occurred in connection with the struggle of Jewish secularizers against both the rabbis and the old habits of tradition. In this drawn-out polemic, religion tended to be downgraded in precisely this manner: in order to contrast the religious doctrine or practice unfavorably with secularism, poor "performance" in the secular area, usually by the imperfectly secularized Jew, was given the mock name of a Jewish religious practice or doctrine, as if to say that the person criticized is still back there in the "primitive" stage. One of the best-known of these gambits, still in use today, is to characterize a story told boringly or drawn out too long as a *megilla,* which actually means scroll, and refers specifically to the Book of Esther. Now clearly the TV performer echoing this kind of inside irony is not engaged in an intramural Jewish *Kulturkampf.* Besides, the secularizers won that battle a long time ago. The performer's interest can only lie in the utilization of the by now routine comic "shock" value of the judiciously placed Yiddish phrase, of which the "tradition" of religious denigration still supplies handy, though obsolete, specimens.

It must indeed be assumed that the laughter provoked by the four Yiddish expressions referred to must be due to the fun the very *sound* of Yiddish manages to evoke, since those expressions are not likely to be understood by most of the audience. Yet it seems unlikely that the Jewish religion, which is the object of these expressions, is not touched by this laughter. There is first of all the immediate association of Yiddish, providing of course its *sound* is recognized, with the Jew, who in turn is associated with what is first of all seen as a *religious* group (cf. the Will Herberg thesis). There are besides also more explicit remarks to be encountered on TV reflecting cavalier Jewish religious attitude ("Frank Sinatra? He's my rabbi." Nov. 12), and sometimes obscurity is carefully removed, as in the instance of *kaddish* ("You know what *kaddish* means." Carson: "Sure. It's the Jewish prayer for the dead." Nov. 8). Clearly, not only Yiddish but Jewish religion is laughed at.

Among the remarks listed there are other examples of Yiddish being used for comic effect. Very typical for the implicit evaluation of Yiddish as such is the "ad lib" by Jack Carter (Nov. 7) when two others are having a short French conversation from which he, not knowing the language, is excluded. He turns to the audience (camera) and says, *"Zei hob'n gezogt . . ."* ("They were saying . . .") as if he's about to translate the French into Yiddish. This juxtaposition of French and Yiddish is a kind of staple in certain types of Jewish-American rhetoric. It is most often found in this form: after a Yiddish word has been used, the phrase is added, "as they say in French." The comic conjunction of the two languages (by Jews) is probably not only due to the felt contrast between the most "strange" and, as it were, the most familiar, but to the apologetic, defensive polarization of the supposedly most "cultured" with the supposedly most scruffy.

Another category emerging from the TV remarks listed

is that of Jewish "foxiness." In George Jessel's story (Nov. 6) the genie foiling the Arab's hostile desires turns out to be Jewish. One might say a foxy Jew has managed to "disguise" himself and thus thwart his enemy. Again, Shecky Greene tells of revealing his "real" name, Shmuel Greenfeld, to the chairman of a Congressional Committee, whereupon the chairman immediately assumes a Yiddish accent (Nov. 6). In other words, a foxy Jew has managed to sneak into the chairman's seat. In the same monologue by Greene, a foxy Jew wangles a restaurant table by jumping the queue and out-tipping the competition. In a serious vein, Truman Capote alludes to Jewish foxiness in referring to a "Jewish literary Mafia" (Nov. 8). Again, in the story by Myron Cohen about the Jew who wants to go to the sun to "look for property, you know, supermarkets" (Nov. 17), a business foxiness is portrayed in the ascribed need to outflank those who are merely going to the moon, though the foxiness is shown up as naivete when the schemer is made to think he can overcome the problem of the sun's heat by going at night. Then there is Merv Griffin's reference to the story about the rabbis present as "relatives of the groom" at the vow-taking ceremony for nuns (Nov. 17), a Jewish story that is something of a foxy "dig" at Christianity. And finally, the attribution by Greene (Nov. 29) of fund-raising foxiness to Moses himself. ("You gotta go. I took out a page in the Bible for it.")

Most of the rest of the Jewish TV material cited represents examples of the inherent comicality of Yiddish, or any reference to Jews. There are two items in which the humor is directed at a concrete, specific situation or event, and which therefore seem no less "valid" than comic TV allusions to general topics. One of these is the remark about Reform rabbis by David Steinberg (Nov. 10), according to which they supposedly write to him asking who Moses and Jezebel are. The point here is of course the remoteness of Reform Judaism from Jewish tradition. An inside remark, really, but clearly comprehensible to all. The other item is Greene's remark that Sammy Davis, a popular Negro singer who has converted to Judaism, has transformed the musical style of his temple's liturgy from "oriental" to jazz (Nov. 29). A reasonable conceit.

On turning to the TV remarks concerning other groups, the Negroes seem at first glance to come closest to the arbitrary comicality of the Jews. "Miracle White?" says Bill Cosby, a Negro comedian, "I'd never buy *that!*" (Nov. 5). The joke turns here on nothing more than Cosby's black complexion. Slappy White, another black comedian, referring to his supposed presence at the Onassis wedding, says, "One of *us* has to be everywhere these days" (Nov. 1). Again, the joke seems to turn merely on White's being a Negro. But there is actually an important difference between Jewish and Negro comicality. Every Negro joke cited is really a tiny shaft hurled in the very real current battle of "liberation." The black comedian is satirizing not himself but the white man. "One of *us* has to be everywhere these days" makes fun not of the Negro but of the white in his haste to prove that his sentiments are impeccably egalitarian. Similarly, the very next remark by White about Duke Ellington having been made an honorary Catholic because of his "rhythm" makes fun of the white cliché *about* the Negro, while also satirizing the Catholic theories of birth control. In Nipsy Russell's remark about the possibility of an antagonized Howard Hughes sending him (Russell) back to Africa, Russell satirizes the limitless power associated with Hughes, and the arbitrary uses such power might be put to. In the light of such interpretations, the remark about never buying Miracle White is only a *partially* tongue-in-cheek expression of black self-assertion.

As to the Catholics, they come off with a much less funny and also a clearly more sympathetic image than the Jews. Some of their raffles may be fakes, but then the parish is very poor (Oct. 31). A dueling Mother Superior (Nov. 8) may be incongruous and funny, but then the incongruous juxtaposition is so totally without echo even in clichés about Catholics (De Sade, for example, charged nuns with fornication, but never with dueling) that the joke seems quite innocuous. And then there is the appearance of Bishop Sheen (Nov. 18), whose function is naturally the creation of a favorable and *serious* image for the church, so that even the jokes he tells reinforce rather than diminish such an image. They go only far enough to accomplish a "humanizing" effect, as in the case of the story about the Pope's remark to a wife killer that he too, had he married, might have killed his wife. The joke by Joe Garagiola (Nov. 26) about St. Christopher having been given to the suddenly successful Mets team has a similar tendency.

Finally, the Italians. There is on the one hand a reference to simple ethnic pride. Merv Griffin: "What about Dean Martin? Don't you like him? He's Italian, like you." Rocky Graziano: "Oh yeah. I'm crazy about Italians . . ." (Nov. 11). A similar note, with only perhaps a touch of benevolent self-irony, is struck by the reference of Kay Ballard to herself as "one crushed Italian," should the building fall (Nov. 13). The one crushed Italian seems less unpleasant certainly than "this old Jew" who stood there, naked, on top of the bed, in George Burns's story about Jack Benny (Nov. 25). The Italians become however less pleasant in Pat Henry's deduction from the night club manager's threatening gestures: "I think they were Italian" (Nov. 26). The joke is nevertheless not simply gratuitous but is meant as a direct reference to the currently topical Mafia.

To recapitulate, the foregoing analysis shows that, in addition to the quantitative preponderance of "Jewish remarks" there is a qualitative difference between the remarks about Jews and those about other groups. The latter remarks are occasionally both serious and noncritical, the former never. (The one "serious" remark about Jews was that by Truman Capote, critical of the "Jewish literary Mafia." Nov. 8) Furthermore the humor about the Jew, unlike that about other groups, is either of the automatic kind, *assuming* the Jew to be funny, or negativistic in evaluation (or self-evaluation). Specifically, this negativism appears in relation to Yiddish, to Jewish religion, and to Jewish inter-personal behavior, which emerges as "foxy."

There now follow the remarks relating to ethnic and/or religious groups heard during a later period: July 20–August 15, 1970 (covering a four-week span). This time only the three late-evening talk shows were monitored and each evening was devoted to just one show, watched from beginning to end. The same sequence of shows for consecutive evenings—Merv Griffin, Tonight, Dick Cavett—was repeated during the entire period. (Since the earlier period, Joey Bishop had been replaced by Dick Cavett.) What was said earlier about deletions applies here also. Again, the remarks concerning Jews are listed first followed by a listing of remarks about other groups.

July 20, 1970   Merv Griffin Show
Al Capp (concerning his mother): When she refused to buy a mink stole, we wondered if she really was Jewish. . . . She was the only Jewish mother who ever refused to go to Florida. (She secretly adopted three European children with her sons' monthly allowance.)

July 21, 1970   Tonight Show
Joan Rivers: In Jewish places I'd do Jewish things . . . You can't lose with those things: *Eli, Eli, Exodus, Yiddishe Mama.* Anybody could do it. Sensational. Would bring the house down. So I came to this place, things were very down, the only single doctor had just left, women wore black wedgies to dinner. So, this boy who went on before me—it was Israel's eighteenth birthday—he put on a *yarmulka*, which is a Jewish prayer hat, and a *talis*, which is a prayer coat, and he sang the three numbers, *Eli, Eli, Exodus,* and *Yiddishe Mama.* It was a sensation. Girls were tossed on stage, had their noses broken, had them fixed again, all without charge. . . . That boy had done *my* act. So I went out, with lots of natural rhythm, and I said, "I'm so glad you liked my husband."

July 23, 1970   Merv Griffin Show
Jack E. Leonard: . . . What's the name of your restaurant. Pippick? That's belly button in Jewish.
Griffin: You Jewish?
Leonard: I started being Jewish 20 minutes ago. . . .

Griffin: . . . Are you ever romantic? I mean, do you have candles?
Leonard: Sure I have candles. I go to synagogue every Friday night. (Big laugh burst from audience.)

July 24, 1970 Tonight Show
Vicki Carr (concerning the Catskill resorts): I don't know quite what to do up there. I'm a *shiksa*, you know.
Dave Berry: A *shiksa*, that's a girl who buys retail. Or you could say it's a razor for females. You know, *Schick*. . . . But you know, what you do up there, when you come out of the dining room you do this (mimes a soundless burp). You know they eat a lot up there. I once had this woman at my table, I'm telling you, she wears a knife and fork on her *charm* bracelet. . . . Moshe Dayan promised to give back the Arab lands, only they're now in his wife's name. . . . (As Ann Corio shows "pasties," which are very small coverings for the nipples of strip teasers) Those are *yarmulkas* for midgets. . . .

July 27, 1970 Dick Cavett Show
Orson Welles: . . . I play an old Jewish professional chess player . . . In the scene I tell the story of Noah . . . I hope that none of my listeners, of whatever faith, will be offended to be reminded that the story of the flood is, after all, a Jewish story . . . (He reads and tells the Noah story in the guise of an old Yiddish-accented man.)

July 28, 1970 Merv Griffin Show
Griffin: . . . What is Tarzan's family name anyway?
Gordon MacRae: Tarzan Schwartz.

July 31, 1970 Merv Griffin Show

Rudy Vallee: ... The rabbi in his car got ahead of the priest and then he approached a red light and stopped. The priest, in his car behind him, had his head in the clouds, thinking of his sermon, and ran smack into the rabbi's car. An Irish cop came alongside, looked into the first car with the rabbi in it, then walked back to the car rammed in behind it, saw the priest and said, "Sure, father, and how fast was he going when he backed into you?

August 4, 1970 Merv Griffin Show

Griffin (to Pat O'Brien): Is your name really Pat O'Brien? If it's Schwartz I'll faint. ...

Meara (of Stiller & Meara, concerning her husband Stiller on an Irish trip): He has that Jewish insanity—everything Irish is holy. He adored everything he saw ... (movies of trip are shown). There's an Irish dog, Irish grass, (a hand on the car wheel appears in the shot) a Jewish hand ... (Now movies of a Spanish trip appear). The bull doesn't like him (Stiller).

Griffin: Maybe he knows he's Jewish.

Meara: Yeah, an anti-Semitic Bull. ...

Stu Gillem: ... It's this boy scout jamboree in Italy. There's a boy from Israel and one from 125th Street in Harlem. "Hey, Moishe," the Harlem kid says, looking at the Vatican, "what's that building?" Little Moishe looks in the guide book. "It says the Pope lives there." "How does he get a job like that?" Moishe looks in the guide book again. "It says the cardinals elect him." "Gee," says the Harlem kid, "I wish the Giants would do the same for Willie Mays." ...

Hans Conreid: There are many waiter stories about Jewish delicatessens. . . . Through the door to the kitchen you can see a whole stack of little plates with coleslaw. Everyone gets one of those. So the waiter brings me a little plate of that coleslaw and whispers, "Don't tell anyone." . . . The customer asks, "Waiter, what time is it?" "It's not my table."

August 6, 1970 Dick Cavett Show
Al Capp: . . . I was with Ted Kennedy before the Catholic Youth Organization . . . I was very cordially received by those Catholic youths.
Dick Cavett: Does that surprise you?
Al Capp: Well I wonder how *he'd* have done at the Bnai Brith

August 8, 1970 Tonight Show (re-run)
Johnny Carson: You know policemen have been dressing up as women to catch muggers in the park. Well, now they're dressing up as rabbis. Rabbis. Really. Till now they've caught three hold-up men, seven muggers, and 400 Arabs. . . .
(to Jan Peerce) I've heard some people thought *Goodbye Columbus* offensive to Jewish people.
Ed McMahon: *I* thought it was.
Jan Peerce: . . . Let me say first, I am a Jew, I am a practicing Jew and I follow as far as I can the laws of our bible and our teachings. . . . I don't want that our people, or any people, should be offended. . . . This movie is not bad for the Jews. It is not only about Jews, it could be about Italians, or Irishmen, or anybody. That's how people behave. My son

(the film's director) respects his people, his parents, his background, and I'm sure *he* wouldn't want to offend them either . . .

August 13, 1970 Dick Cavett Show
Senator Bob Packwood: . . . There are some objections to abortion from Jews as well as Catholics. . . .

Here follow all the remarks heard within the same period concerning other groups:

July 20, 1970 Merv Griffin Show
Zsa Zsa Gabor (concerning her hairdresser): She's a real Hungarian. . . . She believes getting married doesn't mean you can't look at another man. . . .

July 21, 1970 Tonight Show
Joan Rivers: Italian men—there are no gay Italians in Italy. If one is, they make him a hairdresser. They go for anything; they think if it moves and talks, pinch it . . .

July 22, 1970 Dick Cavett Show
Little Negro girls are heard reading their poetry.

July 24, 1970 Tonight Show
Ann Corio: . . . Burlesque, that comes from the Italian.

July 28, 1970 Merv Griffin Show
Maureen O'Sullivan: . . . People have noticed that I've hardly any Irish accent . . . I was brought up in England. . . . When I arrived in Hollywood some publicity men received me with a shillelagh. I had never seen one. You don't see them in Ireland any

more. Then they asked me if I was "lace curtain" or "shanty." I didn't know what that was either. So the rumor started that I wasn't Irish at all. . . . I have relatives in the west of Ireland . . .
Griffin: I have visited relatives there, in a graveyard.
O'Sullivan: It's lovely there, isn't it.
Griffin: Oh yes. But it turned out they had sold the graveyard to the Protestants. I've never heard of selling a graveyard with your relatives in it.

July 31, 1970   Merv Griffin Show
Rudy Vallee: . . . The thief had promised to become a good Catholic, but one day the priest found him with a load of stolen lumber. "Can you make a *novena?*" the priest asked. "I guess so, father," said the thief, "just get me the blueprint and I'll get the lumber for it."
. . . The priest asked her (at confession), "Have you entertained any sinful thoughts?" "No, father," she said, "but they've entertained *me*."
. . . After the service a man went up to the minister and said, "That was a damn good sermon. Yessir, a damn good sermon." The minister said, "Thank you very much, but I wish you wouldn't use that language." "Well," the man said, "I think I have a right to. When the plate was passed I put down a five hundred dollar bill." "The hell you did," said the minister . . .
David Susskind (quoting Bertrand Russell): . . . Women were not supposed to enjoy sex, and it was done only in the dark, and nothing was said. Well, I liked the light, and I liked to talk. My wife was a Philadelphia Quaker. . . . She too finally liked the

light, and then she started to talk, and in the end she was no longer a Quaker.

August 4, 1970 Merv Griffin Show
Pat O'Brien: . . . The priest was saying, "Every man in this parish must die one day." A little man kept laughing. Finally the priest asked him, "And why are you laughing?" "I'm not from this parish," the little man said.
. . . The priest was asking each one separately, "You want to go to heaven?" "Yes." "You want to go to heaven?" "Yes." "You want to go to heaven?" "Not particularly." "You mean to say," the priest asked, "when you die you don't want to go to heaven?" "Oh," the man said, "you didn't say anything about dying. I thought you want me to come along *today*."
Griffin (to Arthur Treacher): You want to go to heaven?
Treacher: How can I? I'm an Episcopalian.
Griffin: Oh yes, that's right. We don't let Episcopalians in.
O'Brien: You know what an Episcopalian is? It's a Catholic who flunked Latin . . .
Stu Gillem (black comedian): A little colored boy was spanked by his parents because he put a sheet over his head and made believe he was joining the KKK. . . . After he stopped crying, the little boy said, "Ain't it a shame. I'm only in the KKK five minutes and already I hate you colored people!"

August 5, 1970 Tonight Show
Martin Braverman: . . . The tough kid in school, Salvator Garagonzoli, ten years old and paying child support, came to school every day with a new stolen car. He sold us insurance—"For what?"—Pow! When he grad-

uated they gave him not a diploma but a gold watch, with the text of the Geneva Convention in back . . .
Peter Boyle: . . . For a while I was a Christian Brother, you know, they make the wine. . . . After a while I saw there wasn't any money in it, you didn't get to meet any girls. . . . I was a maitre d'. . . . You have to be very Prussian, you need a strong will, you have to intimidate people: Haf you rrrelatiffs in Stuttgart?

August 8, 1970   Tonight Show (rerun)
Billy Graham: . . . Just call me Billy. In England, you know, the Archbishop is called "My Lord," or "Your Grace," and one day he was visiting a school. . . . He asked the boy how old he is and the boy was scared to death. So he said, "Ten, My God.". . . . (He then talks seriously of Christianity.)
Biff Rose (in monologue about a southern Negro who never went to church): . . . He said, when asked by the white preacher what he believed in, that "man is beholden to his neighbor without the hope of heaven or the fear of hell! . . . "Serves him right," the white folks said when they saw him hang, "he had no religion."

August 11, 1970   Merv Griffin Show
Merv Griffin: And now, we have Miss Universe. . . . As you know, Monte Rock is from Puerto Rico. Well, so is Miss Universe . . .
Monte Rock: Puerto Ricans are beautiful people . . .

Upon analysis, the data of this second period may be said to bear out the results obtained in the first. The one significant difference between earlier and later period is the occurrence in the latter of several remarks about Jews which are both "serious" and non-critical. (Orson Welles, July 27, Jan Peerce, August 8, Senator Packwood, August 13). Since two of these, (Welles, Packwood) are from the Dick Cavett Show, which had replaced The Joey Bishop Show of the first period, and since only *one* comic Jewish remark (Al Capp, August 6) occurred on that show, it must be assumed that much depends on who hosts these shows. However, there was still a great preponderance of humorous remarks about Jews. To be precise, there were twelve humorous Jewish "occasions" compared to thirteen humorous occasions for all other groups combined. (This includes one item listed in the Jewish section which also concerns the Irish [Rudy Vallee, July 31], as well as one concerning the Christian Brothers.) Again, also, the humor about Jews largely either suggested arbitrariness (Gordon MacRae, July 28, Merv Griffin, August 4, Meara, August 4, Al Capp, August 6) or made use of the comicality of Yiddish or Jewish religion (Joan Rivers, July 21, Jack E. Leonard, July 23, Dave Berry, July 24) or dealt with Jewish foxiness (Dave Berry, July 24; Hans Conreid, August 4). However, there were also comical suggestions of other Jewish failings: sybaritism (Al Capp, July 20) and gluttony (Dave Berry, July 24).

Of the other groups, no single one had more than *two* comic occasions. As to the kind of humor involved, the items concerning Protestants and Catholics (Rudy Vallee, July 31, Pat O'Brien, August 4) do not satirize religion as such, but rather the "little man" who cannot live up to high religious standards. These religious jokes, unlike the Jewish kind, do not represent an anti-religious point of view but come rather from within religion. As to humor concerning ethnic groups, the two Italian items both have negative connotations. In one (Joan Rivers, July 21) Italians are all represented as satyrs, and in the other (Martin Braverman, August 5) the budding high school gangster is Italian. These findings support the findings of the earlier period: the humor about the two major religions is "supportive"; the humor about Italians is not always innocuous.

Another critical comic item is the one about Prussianism and its association with a menacing attitude (Peter Boyle, August 5). The rest of the items are either serious or benignly comical, with evangelist Billy Graham offsetting his own humor by his own seriousness.

The second period of television watching thus confirms the earlier conclusion that of all groups the Jews are given by far the most comic presentation, and that this humor is based either on an automatic assumption that Jewishness is funny or on several alleged negative characteristics. These negativist aspects detract from what has been called an "ultimate" Jewish Comic Image on TV. That is to say, the Jew is not only shown as a *gratuitously* funny figure. Nevertheless, a major portion of the Jewish humorous material cited utilizes the Jewish Comic Image, since the items apparently critical of Yiddish and Jewish religion have in fact no other intention than such utilization.

BOOKS

THE BOOK PUBLISHING FIELD REVEALS A KIND OF DOUBLE standard in the approach to Jewish subject matter that shows up very clearly in book publicity. An aura of solemnity distinguishes the ads of a certain type of Jewish book, such as James Michener's *The Source,* or Abba Eban's *My People,* or Elie Wiesel's *Beggar in Jerusalem.* And indeed these and others like them are "serious" books; they deal in religion, history, romance, but not humor. Probably not a hint is there in any of them of even the possibility of a Jewish Comic Image. But it might be noted that of such serious popular books about Jews only a remarkably small number (such as the recent *The Chosen* and its sequel, *The Promise,* by Chaim Potok) deal with *American* Jews.

On the other hand, a lot of publicity for Jewish books, whether comic or not, reveals a tendency to meet a presumed reader *expectation* of humor. James Jaffe's sociological study entitled *The American Jews* is announced as a "tough, humorous, human book about American Jews . . ." (*The New York Times,* December 13, 1968). And here is some random gossip concerning the publicity of other books from a publishing magazine: "Its ad agency submitted, and Crown, the publishers, initially agreed to publish an advertisement with the headline 'A funny thing happened to the Jew on the way to the gas ovens,' for the book *They Fought Back*, about the Jews' underground war against Hitler. An overground war at Crown produced a new headline, 'An unexpected thing happened on the way to the gas ovens,'" (*Books*, April 1967). Or another item from the same issue: "Ads for *Erotica Judaica* will carry the headline '. . . Why is this night different from all other nights?' And the copy line 'This is the first documented account of the significant role that sex played in the development and destiny of the Jews. Who would have guessed?'" (*ibid.*)

A similarly jaunty tone concerning the juxtaposition of Jews and sex occurs in the blurb of the pocket book edition of *Chewsday* by Dan Greenburg (N. Y., 1969): "It should have been billed as a Jewish sex novel since all the interesting characters in it seem to be Jewish. Greenburg disowns this parochial view. There is nothing in this book that gentiles don't do also. . . . And so good bye to Myra Breckenridge (obviously gentile), John Updike (obviously gentile), Candy (ditto), here come Marvin and Laura Breitfeller and Stanley and Mandy Apple, a real switch."

Then there are the *outright* comic Jewish books, and these are advertised with outright comic ads. Thus: "Think Jewish! Get on the bandwagon before it's too late with Albert Vorspan's uproariously funny guide to everything from 'How to escape Jewish Fund-raising' (you should live so long) to 'How to be a Jewish liberal.' *My Rabbi Doesn't Make House Calls*, A Guide to Games Jews Play." (The New York *Times*, July 24, 1969). This type of comic Jewish book has become a staple in American book publishing; its most successful recent example is probably *How to Be a Jewish Mother* (Dan Greenburg), which was for a while on top of the non-fiction list of 1965. This brief, mildly benevolent mock-pedantic treatise that, judged by its contents, should perhaps more honestly have been entitled "How to Be a Middle-class Mother" (but would then presumably not have found a publisher) was followed by other comic treatises, such as the heavily advertised *What's a Jewish Girl?* (Lyn Tornabene, 1966), which should, if honest, have been entitled "What's an Over-sheltered Neurotic Girl?" (with, presumably, equally negative commercial consequences). By the time of the 1967 war in Israel, the market was certainly prepared to receive not only such comic exploitations of things Jewish as a widely seen poster showing a spindly Superman with Chassidic beard and black hat, but such hastily spawned books as *Blintzkrieg* and *Irving of Arabia*. Curiously, the very events refuting the stereotype of Jewish inability to fight served as occasion for the stereotype's reiteration.

Most probably the novel is a more important type of literary vehicle for the Jewish Comic Image than the farcical monograph, more important because it is the nature of the genre to make a claim to seriousness, even when comic. According to Charles Angoff (50) the "big push" for Jewish themes in current American novels was supplied by Herman Wouk's *Marjorie Morningstar* in 1955, a book that Angoff accuses of not containing "one recognizable character" and of setting the tone for the comic exploitation of Jewishness. Certainly there have been since then numerous novels of Jewish content and humorous mood, though that mood may have different tones of voice, for instance a tolerantly indulgent one, as in Herbert Tarr's *Heaven Help Us* (1968), or a recklessly disdainful one, as in Philip Roth's *Portnoy's Complaint* (1969). What is common to such novels is the implication that even if considered thoroughly and at some length—even, that is, if it warrants the writing of a novel—Jewishness does not provoke, or perhaps merit, a treatment commensurate with its intrinsic claims, i.e. the serious claims of Judaism and the claim of a Jewish sub-culture in America to a "normalized" status, equal to that of other religious and/or ethnic groups.

Alfred Kazin, in discussing an earlier period of Jewish literary creativity in America (54), lists a number of typical works from the early thirties, such as Henry Roth's *Call it Sleep,* Michael Gold's *Jews Without Money,* Daniel Fuchs's *Summer in Williamsburg.* These books, according to Kazin, contained an "awareness of the Jew as a new force" on the American scene. And there was a passionate need in these writers "just out of the city ghettos" to come to terms with both the ancient experience transmitted by their immigrant parents and the American scene they were facing. "There are experiences so extreme," says Kazin, "that, after living them, one can do nothing with them *but* put them into words." These writers of the thirties, according to Kazin, recorded the extreme experience of living on the frontier between two worlds with a seriousness that amounted to passion. And Jewishness, as embodied in the European parents, was a force to be reckoned with, so that even if there was rejection, the ultimate respect of passionate seriousness was paid.

Of course it must be kept in mind that these novels of life in the ghetto of the American city reflected the encounter of the son with the Jewish *immigrant* father (and mother), whose Jewishness was a reasonably intact tradition, even after that ocean crossing. By contrast, the

American Jewish novelist of the sixties records most often the encounter with an *American* Jewish middle-class parent (more likely the mother, since the father is concentrating his energies on making a living rather than molding the young), whose Jewishness has become incidental, if not irrelevant, to him or herself. Thus, the father of Stern, in Bruce Jay Friedman's *Stern,* is "self-conscious on the subject" and has "great fun with such phrases as 'orange Jews' and 'grapefruit Jews.' When Stern would say, 'I heard that, Dad,' his father would say, 'Yeah, but I'll bet you never heard prune Jews.'" (25, p. 45) This is about all Stern has to report of his father's "Jewishness." The experience of such an enfeebled kind of heritage does not engender passion, or even seriousness.

On the other hand, it is accordingly not surprising that in *Herzog,* by Saul Bellow, a novel on the best-seller lists of 1964 and 1965 which deals with the immigrant experience, Jewishness "emerges solidly, naturally, authentically, from the family experiences that [Herzog] remembers so vividly" (95), and that Jewishness "functions . . . as the main province of [the hero's] temperament" (*ibid.*). Herzog thinks back to life on Napoleon Street, in the Jewish ghetto of Montreal, and he remembers "the bootlegger's boys reciting ancient prayers," and he thinks—"Here was a wider range of human feelings than he had ever again been able to find." (*Herzog,* quoted in 95).

Possibly it is precisely the lack of such a range of human feelings that writers like Friedman and Roth perceive as they contemplate current American Jewish life. There is neither the bootlegging nor the ancient prayers. The immigrants' offspring have moved up the social scale and have left the intense struggles with life and also with God behind them. Acculturation has flattened out the contours of existence. It is a somewhat bleak but not uncomfortable scene the son remembers as he writes of it. He can only protest with a giggle, for even as an adult he has retained that early feeling about Jewishness as a kind of intrusion, with occasional mildly unpleasant consequences in the gentile world. (When Stern in uniform is accosted with exaggerated floridity by a blustery drunk at a bar as a "fighting Jew," he has to struggle very hard to convince himself that the drunk may mean it in the sense of "fighting Swede.") The writer betrays the very irrelevancy of that intrusion even at the moment of writing about it: Stern's Hebrew School teacher, writes Friedman, has cast him "as the wicked Egyptian king, Ahasuerus, in a Purim play" (25, p. 44), and Friedman does not bother to research the fact (since it is he, in his own voice, that is doing the historical identifying) that that king is really Persian. Friedman, the writer, is as casually unengaged about what he is writing as the boy Stern was in what he was experiencing.

It would accordingly seem then that the comedy found in so much Jewish popular writing is the natural outcome of an experience that did not have the making of genuine passion or seriousness in it. But the real object of the comedy is then not Jewishness, it having been largely *absent,* but the middle-class way of life. Roth's Portnoy complains that he is, at 33, still in the grip of his parents: "Watch out! Don't do it! Alex—no!" (83, p. 35). But isn't the supposed freedom juxtaposed against this sense of restriction contained in the memory of those apparently less heavily supervised Catholic kids of the *working class?* Portnoy rants (in capital letters) "You Jewish mothers are just too much to bear!" and goes on, "I have read

Freud on Leonardo, Doctor . . . What do we want, me . . . and Leonardo? To be left alone!" Was Leonardo's mother Jewish also?

There thus seems to be more *ado* made about Jewishness in the comic novel than the subject, judging by the interior evidence of the novels themselves, warrants. The authors are often describing American middle-class style, but tag that style "Jewish." True, most American Jews *are* middle-class, but the novels practically suggest that only the Jews are middle-class, that middle-class style means Jewish style. Perhaps at least partial explanation of this playing up of "Jewish" lies in the need for hyperbole and shock effect (a sense of taboo still clinging to Jewish subject matter), which are indispensable to the comic's equipment. Roth's novel, a 1969 best-seller, is in fact put in the form of a comic monologue, though not delivered by a stand-up comic but by a supine analysand. Yet this device excuses the substitution of sensationalism for sensibility. The events of a childhood in Newark (or bachelorhood in Manhattan) are not filtered through the fine grid of an "author's" sensitive perception but rumble through the hand-mike, one might say, of the narrator's eccentricity. Thus, gags take the place of insight: ". . . my mother is on the phone for days at a stretch and has to be fed intravenously, her mouth is going at such a rate about her Alex" (83, p. 106). And it is, incidentally, also possible for the author to hedge upon the narrator's pronouncements concerning, for example, Judaism, not only because the narrator is after all supposed to be something of a "nut," but also through the narrator's self-ironization. Here he is talking with the voice of his adolescent self: "Good Christ, mother, the whole world knows already, *so why don't you? Religion is the opiate of the people!* . . . I happen to believe in the rights of man, rights such as are extended in the Soviet Union to *all* people, regardless of race, religion, and color. My communism, in fact, is why I now insist on eating with the cleaning lady" (*ibid*). A little later he says: "I will not treat any human being (outside my family) as inferior" (*ibid*). Portnoy caricatures his own blindness as well as his own naiveté.

The intentions behind the attitudes in Roth's book are thus blurred, and the impression is reinforced that the comedy is not meant to serve the remarks on Jewishness, but vice versa. The sense that the conflict with Jewishness is "souped up" is in fact borne out by the laugh-shock-laugh-shock treatment of sexuality. Here are two subjects, Jewishness and sex, ideally suited to popular titillation.

In direct conjunction the two subjects serve to heighten the comic shock effect of each other. Thus, Friedman introduces the following Seder scene, but one in which scatology takes the place of sex: Uncle Mackie, who flies in each year from Arizona for the family Seder, "would take Stern around the waist, pull him close and whisper confidentially, 'I just want to find out something. Do you still make peepee in your pants?' And then he would explode with laughter, until he checked himself, held his side, and said, 'I've got to do something about the plumbing.' He continued the peepee inquiries long into Stern's teens. When the Seder began, Uncle Sweets would take long difficult passages to himself . . . but soon Uncle Mackie, warming to the Seder, would break in with great clangor . . . Before long, Uncle Sweets would stop and say to him 'What the hell do you know? You shit in your hat in Phoenix.' And Uncle Mackie would fly at him, saying 'I'll kick your two-bit ass through the window' . . . Toward the tail end of the Seder, Stern and his cousin Flip would sneak off to the bedroom, get a dictionary, and look up dirty words, such as 'vulva' and 'pudendum.' They would then open their flies and compare pubic hair growths . . ." (25, p. 46). Or Stern, as soldier, is invited to dinner after a visit to a synagogue in a strange town by an "orthodox watchmaker who had a large and bovine daughter named Naomi. . . . When Stern had finished dinner, he was left alone with the girl in a parlor that smelled of aged furniture, unchanged since it had been brought across from Albania after a pogrom. The light was subdued and Stern, belly bursting with chopped liver and noodle pudding, swiftly got her breasts out. . . . Stern imagined himself piercing her and thereby summoning up the wrath of ancient Hebrew gods, ones who would sleep benignly as long as he stayed above the waist" (*ibid.*, p. 57).

Perhaps in an attempt to heighten the potency of the mixture, Friedman adds, in *A Mother's Kisses* (1964), the Jewish Mother, who combines Jewishness, sex (she is pictured as a sensual type, at least in her talk), and status as erstwhile sacred cow. Friedman's portrait, however, emerges as a sketch of a real individual, not a prototype. She is comic, of course, but by virtue of *her* rather than the narrator's sense of humor. The intonation is Jewish: "All right, where were you that I wasn't allowed to hear a voice on a telephone? That it wasn't important enough that I be contacted?" (27) And she is something of a stand-up comic: (To a policeman who has just told her son not to "sass" his mom) "That's all right, officer, . . . I feel that I have a very smart son in college who suddenly developed public speaking. I don't have a boy any more, I have Winston Churchill." (27, p. 278) But the Jewishness and the comedy combine to help round out the character and there is a sense of authenticity.

There is, on the other hand, the Jewish Mother of *Portnoy's Complaint,* which is worth a somewhat closer look not only because its Jewish comedy seems to lie closer to the arbitrariness of the Jewish Comic Image than to the idiosyncrasy of character, but because it was, as a best-seller, an important "cultural fact" of 1969. Apparently, the novel's intention—to portray the Jewish Mother as a new culture monster—has found considerable resonance in the public imagination.

Now while it is true that the status of the Jewish Mother has declined since the era of "sainthood" associated with the strains of "A Yiddishe Mamma," the Jewish Mother of the comparatively recent *How to Be a Jewish Mother* was nevertheless only a rather harmless *nudnick,* complicating adolescent life with unwanted sandwiches. And certainly in the thirties, though the Freudian castrator image must have been fresh among American intellectuals, American Jewish novelists did not downgrade her. "In the beginning," writes Kazin concerning those writers, "there was the Jewish mother and her son, but the son grew up, he went out into the world, he became a writer. That was the beginning of his career, and usually the end of the novel. Jews don't believe in original sin, but they certainly believe in the original love that they knew in the *shtetl,* in the kitchen, in the Jewish household." (54) Now if there is no apparent love in Portnoy for his mother, the distinction made above between immigrant and American parents might be invoked in explanation: perhaps the immigrant mother radiated love, while the American mother can only induce eating in her children by hovering over them (as Mrs. Portnoy is described as doing) with knife in hand. Yet there are in Portnoy's monologue a sufficient number of *allusions* to motherly love to indicate that this is not the case. What does happen is that the narrator's comic mode, all through his book-length monologue, is only useful in spotlighting moments of oppression; there is just no comedy in moments of gentle affection: "While I crayon a picture of her, she showers—and now in the sunshine of her bedroom, she's dressing to take me downtown. She sits on the edge of the bed in her padded bra and her girdle, rolling on her stockings and chattering away. Who is Mommy's good little boy? Who is the best little boy a mommy ever had? Who does mommy love more than anything in the whole wide world? I am absolutely punchy with delight, and meanwhile follow in their tight, slow, agonizingly delicious journey up her legs the transparent stockings . . ." (83, p. 43) And so the scene becomes the occasion for comic bravura concerning incestuous lusts.

It is of course in the nature of comic monologues to draw one-dimensional pictures, and that is precisely what Roth does, in order to make easy laughs possible. Huge chunks of reality, and feeling, are withheld. In contrast, here is Herzog encountering a stray memory: "Leaving the cab, he thought how his mother would moisten her handkerchief at her mouth and rub his face clean. He had no business to recall this. . . . But he had not forgotten the odor of his mother's saliva on the handkerchief that summer morning. . . . All children have cheeks and all mothers spittle to wipe them tenderly. These things either matter or they do not matter. It depends on the universe, what it is." (9, p. 46) Portnoy lives of course in a universe different from Herzog's, though it is only that of the comic momentum of his monologue. It seems likely that the resonance found by this monologue in the interested response of a wide public is of that especially hollow kind that accompanies the gag-filled monologues of comedians, where the audience responds not to well-considered insights but to humorous titillations.

It might be instructive to juxtapose Portnoy's Jewish Mother with a gentile mother in a recent *New Yorker* story (76). Here, once more, is Mrs. Portnoy: "Open your mouth. Why is your throat red? Do you have a headache you're not telling me about? You're not going to any baseball game, Alex, until I see you move your neck. Is your neck stiff? Then why are you moving it that way? You act like you were nauseous, are you nauseous?" (83, p. 32) Now the gentile mother: "She watched over every step I took and every breath I drew. Between her terror that I would get pneumonia for running too fast and the suspicion that a contact with the gardener's children would give me lice, or that through the friendliness of a Rumanian officer, who put me in the saddle of his horse, I would get syphillis, I did not develop into a very social youngster. In wintertime, on the big public skating rink, I found myself lonely in a corner . . . an enormous woolen shawl wrapped six times around my neck, while all around a whirl of hilarious liveliness filled the sparkling winter day." (76) And now Portnoy, facetiously, about *his* ice-skating: "In winter, when the polio germs are hibernating and I can bank upon surviving outside of an iron lung until the end of the school year, I ice-skate on the lake in Irvington Park. . . . I skate round and round in circles behind the *shikses* who live in Irvington. . . . I am ecstatic . . . a nosegay of *shikses,* a garland of gentile girls . . . skating behind the puffy red earmuffs and the fluttery yellow ringlets of a strange *shikse* teaches me the meaning of the word *longing.* It is almost more than an angry thirteen-year-old little Jewish Momma's Boy can bear." (83, p. 142) But here again is that over-protected gentile boy, also on the ice, also longing for the different: "The majority of the young skaters were Jews. Among them were some extremely pretty girls, with whom, one by one, I clandestinely fell in love, suffering not only from the over-protectiveness of my mother but from guilt. My mother came to fetch me every day, and, in spite of my violent protests, had me wrapped in blankets and furs in order to protect my frail health after the exhausting exercise. My departure had become a public amusement so humiliating that I did not dare to look the Jewish girls in the eye even when my mother had not yet turned up." (76) Clearly, both Portnoy and this Austrian Catholic boy are reciting similar versions of *Civilization and its Discontents,* a title in fact appropriated from Freud for an excerpt of Roth's book that appeared in *New American Review #3,* 1968. It is not *Jewish* civilization that is at issue. But Roth can count on an audience conditioned to laugh at the American Jew; the other author (Gregor von Rezzori) has no Austrian Catholic equivalent.

By contrast, another popular novel, *Heaven Help Us,* by Herbert Tarr (1968), while also comically negative about Jews, directs its aim carefully at the suburbanite temple-goers who imagine they are the genuine article. In this respect, at least, it invokes an aspect of an older, "authentic," Jewish humor whose purpose was the making of the "better" Jew. The narrator is a young rabbi who assumes his first post with a surburban congregation, wanting only "to learn, and teach others and . . . do justice, love mercy, and to walk humbly with God" (97, p. 4). What he finds is a group of business-minded, status-conscious hedonists whose perplexed silence at the rabbi's mention of the word "God" suggests that they are waiting for God's family name. The synagogue, run as if it were a competitive business concern, turns out to have been built only because the Jewish kids looked silly Sunday mornings, having no place to go while the gentile kids went to church or Sunday School. Gentile questions began to be heard and so the formation of a congregation was decided upon. The young rabbi is hired, among other extraneous reasons, because of his non-Jewish looks and his resemblance to Harry Belafonte. The theme of the book is the fruitless struggle of the rabbi to institute programs of "adult education" and "social action" in the face of a congregation interested only in bagel-and-lox brunches, weenie roasts, the bowling league, the fund drive for an enlarged temple kitchen, the temple musical *My Fair Sadie*. While the Jews depicted are mostly unpleasant caricatures, their constant juxtaposition by the author with the rabbi's upright stance leaves a final impression of Jewry-gone-to-pot, but measured by the standard of the Jewish "idea" itself. And so, if the Jews come out heavily tainted by the comedy, Jewishness does not.

Measuring the "authenticity" of humor by its relation to an actual, internally authenticated social reality, the book by Tarr, unlike those by Friedman and Roth, is an authentic comedy about American Jews, reflecting and commenting on a real social situation. Yet the fact that the book, which deals with a rather parochial, intra-mural Jewish problem, became a national best-seller suggests that here too the broader, fashionable association of Jews and comedy may play a role. To be sure, the association is not arbitrarily exploited *within* the book, but it is so exploited in the selling of the book, which is offered as still *another* comedy about Jews than which, the implication goes, hardly anything could be more comic. A trade ad by Random House includes the following: "... you'll recognize the entire Gewalt Gestalt from the Temple right down to the Posh Nosh Delicatessen ... caters to a wide audience, the whole *mishpochah* plus just about any true believer in entertainment" (*Publishers Weekly*, February 19, 1968). Moreover, there is in fact evidence within the book itself that the author, not surprisingly, was aiming for this wide appeal and willing, for its sake, to sacrifice some integrity. For the rabbi-hero drops an occasional remark most incongruous for a character shown otherwise to be rather learned in Judaism and leaning toward orthodoxy. Thus, "if I declined to invoke [pronounce an invocation] here, the trustees were liable to think me a *goy* or something, maybe even the anti-Christ" (97, p. 6)—a thought not likely to occur even ironically to such a character, unless thinking of the *goyish* audience.

Still another genre of Jewish comedy in the novel is represented by Mark Mirsky's *Thou Worm, Jacob* (1967). Its characters might be described as neo-Aleichem, being old East European Jews, poor, quaint, and at odds with modernity in their thorough allegiance to the old tradition. But they are located in present-day Boston and their kind is dying out. The old men have trouble assembling a *minyan* (quorum of ten) for prayers and decide eventually that, since the old horse pulling the wagon they've been riding in is "circumcised," they can use him as a tenth "man." At the *finale* the men are praying while the horse's head sticks in through the synagogue window. This *bizarrerie* goes of course beyond the realistic comedy of Sholom Aleichem. The laughter here takes on overtones of pathetic absurdity, overpowering the very milieu depicted. The Jew is blown up into a symbol, a Cosmic Clown, the essence of the Human Comedy. A similar "metaphysical" patina also lies over the comedy of such "authentically" Jewish writers as Isaac B. Singer, who writes mostly of the *shtetl*, and Bernard Malamud. These writers bestow an aura of philosophical dignity upon the association of the Jew with comedy, yet the association is nevertheless there.

The reference to the novels by Tarr and Mirsky serves to show the existence of comic Jewish novels diverging from those that rather arbitrarily feature the urban "antihero" as comic Jew, of which the novels of Friedman and Roth are good examples. Yet the latter genre is a dominant one in the field (other random examples are *A Bad Man* [Stanley Elkin, 1967], *Baby hip* [Patricia Welles, 1967], *Move!* [Joel Lieber, 1968], *Up* [Ronald Sukenick, 1968]), and it would seem that at least subtly those comic Jewish novels whose humor is more integral to character and situation do share in the "boom" of this literature dominated by the humor of the Jewish Comic Image. At the same time it must be noted that the area of books is the only one of the four media surveyed that also noticeably displays an image of the "serious" Jew. Many Jewish titles, some widely read, are published each year that are not comic, and so the *overall* Jewish image in books is not so unequivocally comic as it is in the other media.

Nevertheless, there is no other group that gets as much comic attention, even in books, as the Jews. The publishers' lists show no comic essays like *How to Be a Jewish Mother* about non-Jewish groups. There is also no fashion of comic novels about any such groups. Catholic fiction, for instance, is serious, although there are exceptions, like *Powdered Eggs* (Charles Simmons, 1964), whose clown-ish Catholic hero recounts such tales as his confessing before his priest to every conceivable sin and then, in response to the Father's barely concealed shock, revealing as still another sin his incorrigible tendency to lie. This character's attitude to his religion is expressed in statements like "my Catholic but otherwise human mother . . ." (92, p. 102). This is probably less damning however than Portnoy's implied "my Jewish and therefore inhuman mother." But homage to the Jewish Comic Image is apparently paid even here, in Catholic precincts: the Jewish girlfriend of the hero asks him whether he wouldn't want to become circumcised "for me," and the hero responds by running into the bathroom for some water and pouring it upon the nude female in bed, indicating that she has now been baptized, is no longer Jewish, and thus no longer in need of a circumcised male.

If this incorporation of the Jewish Comic Image humor into the Catholic novel is a kind of testimonial to the importance of the Image, perhaps its crucial place in a novel by the "Wasp" author John Updike is a veritable obeisance to it. In *Bech: a Book* (1970) Updike probes the life of a Jewish writer whose writing "block" is turned by Updike into a symbol of *shlemiel*hood. This Bech is supposedly a serious writer, a representative of the current literary "Jewish renaissance," a composite of, among others, Bellow, Malamud, Mailer, and Salinger, as Bech himself "says" in the Foreword. His model (or models) is thus very much a part of cultural reality and therefore he is not necessarily just a pretext for an exercise in Jewish Comic Imagery. Yet Updike often tends to make him precisely that. The following scene, an admittedly flagrant example, is set in Bech's childhood. Bech's mother has come to pick him up from school, where, she suspects, he is too interested in the gentile girls:

> "You know I don't like your coming into the school."
> "Mister Touch-Me-Not," she said, "so ashamed of his mother he wants all his blue-eyed *shiksas* to think he came out from under a rock, I suppose. Or better yet, lives in a tree like Siegfried."
> Somewhere in the past she had wormed out of him his admiration of the German girls at school. He blushed. "Thanks to you," he told her, "they're all two years older than me."
> "Not in their empty golden heads, they're not so old. Maybe in their pants, but that will come to you soon enough. Don't hurry the years, soon enough they'll hurry you."
> Homily, flattery, and humiliation: these were what his mother applied to him, day after day, like a sculptor's pats. It deepened his blush to hear her mention Eva Hassel's pants. Were they what would come to him soon enough? This was her style, to mock his reality and stretch his expectations. "Mother, don't be fantastic."
> "Ai, nothing fantastic. There's nothing one of these golden girls would like better than fasten herself to some smart little Jewish boy. Better that than some sausage-grinding Fritz who'll go to beer and beating her before he's twenty-five. You keep your nose in your books."
> "That's where it was. Where are you taking me?"
> "To see something more important than where to put your *putz*."
> "Mother, don't be vulgar."
> "Vulgar, that's what I call a boy who wants to put his mother under a rock. His mother and his people and his brain, all under a rock." (99, pp. 174–175)

This is of course not imitation of life, but imitation of Mrs. Portnoy, or of Portnoy himself. Brazen talk before her little boy of girls' "pants" and of his *"putz"* is probably about as authentic in the Jewish mother as discussion of Gefilte Fish is in a New England matriarch. Moreover, the speech pattern is itself curiously false: ". . . better that than some sausage-grinding Fritz who'll go to beer and beating her before he's twenty-five." No New York Jewess, which is what Mrs. Bech supposedly is, ever said these words. To be sure, Updike may simply not know the idiom, but falseness is probably unavoidable in any case if the aim is not so much depiction of reality as utilization of a fashionable comic image.

SUMMARY OF MEDIA SURVEY

TWO CRITERIA WERE SET FOR DETERMINING THE PRESENCE of a Jewish Comic Image: 1) a more comic overall image for Jews than for other groups; 2) the prevalence of "arbitrariness" in the Jewish humor. The results obtained show that there are differences only in degree to which the several media meet the two conditions.

The weakest overall comic image of the Jew (though it is still stronger than that of any other group) seems to emerge in books, despite the huge impact of a comic book like *Portnoy's Complaint,* and despite the existence of a genre of ephemeral comic "treatises" about Jews which does not exist about other groups. For there are widely read novels in which Jews, even American Jews, are treated seriously (Potok, Bellow). As to the character of the humor in the comic novels, several examples were found in which the comedy of the Jew may be said to be "valid" rather than arbitrary (Mirsky, Tarr). On both points of evaluation, books, collectively, showed a higher incidence of non-complying items than the other media, so that books may be characterized as the least effective propagators of the Jewish Comic Image.

It is more difficult to order theatre and TV in a hierarchy of importance in relation to the problem. In the theatre, compliance with the first condition is nearly perfect, since the treatment of Jews, unlike that of other groups, is almost totally comic. However, a significant, though minor, segment of the plays does not meet the second condition of arbitrariness. In TV, on the other hand, the Jewish humor is mostly arbitrary (though there were some examples of humor directed at specific "failings"), but among the rather large total of Jewish references there also appear a number of serious items. In passing, it might also be mentioned that a case might be made for the existence of a minor Italian comic image (minor certainly in relation to the sheer number of Jewish items) which is explicitly unflattering at times.

Films, finally, meet almost perfectly both criteria for a Jewish Comic Image, since Jews were found to be singled out for comedy and only one of the films (*The Angel Levine*) presents the American Jew with pathos as well as comedy. Furthermore, it was only this film, and to some extent another (*The Producers*), which did not live up to the second condition involving arbitrariness.

To recapitulate, while there are differences between the media, each must be said to meet the two conditions set for establishing the existence of a Jewish Comic Image in the popular culture.

II
The Historical Background of the Jewish Comic Image

INTRODUCTION

IN THE FOLLOWING SECTION AN ATTEMPT IS MADE TO outline the historical background of the Jewish Comic Image in America. To accomplish this one has to turn to Jewish rather than to American history, for the association of the Jew with comedy did not suddenly begin upon his arrival in New York Harbor. In Europe as well the Jew not only had his own repertoire of jokes—as have members of every other group—but he had an especially close connection with comedy, both as its butt and as its creator, in the eyes of non-Jews. By the 19th century the jokes of anti-Semites blended and often became interchangeable with the jokes of Jews and Jewish humorists, resulting in a European Jewish image probably no less comic than it was unsympathetic.

As will, however, be shown, the Jews are not a "naturally" comic people; that is, they do not have a long history of self-irony. It seems more correct to say that from as far back as biblical times down to nearly the beginning of the 19th century, to judge by the available evidence, they were a rather humorless people. If one can speak of a Jewish "temperament," a residue perhaps of Mediterranean personality distinguished by a certain vitality and capacity for "passion," that temperament was expended down those many centuries not on humor but on tenacious self-assertion and religiosity. Laughter was, if anything, rather frowned upon. Only a drastic change in historical circumstances finally diverted that temperament to irony —more significantly self-irony—of a force explosive enough to affect European humor itself.

By thus going back to examine the social context of the origins of the Jewish Comic Image it becomes possible to assess, by comparison, its present American context. Is this context, one can then ask, a "valid" one for the Image? Or conversely, it becomes possible, in the light of its original context, to assess the meaning of the Image. Is this meaning, it can then be asked, a valid one in the present context? The answers should provide insights into the reasons for the existence of that Image in America today.

Needless to say, what follows is not a history of Jewish humor, but rather an attempt to relate data of Jewish history to the changing importance and meaning of humor in Jewish life. The major part of the historical data is derived from Graetz (34) for Germany, and Dubnow (22) for Eastern Europe, although other histories were also consulted. Various collections of Jewish humor were utilized. The introduction to one of these, Salcia Landmann, *Der Jüdische Witz* (60), has proved very useful in its perspective on the sociology of European Jewish humor.

THE HUMOR OF EARLY TIMES

IN ATTEMPTING TO TRACE THE ASSOCIATION OF HUMOR WITH Jewishness back to its earliest manifestations one discovers that there is no evidence that the ancient Jews, both of the biblical and post-biblical eras, were a "humorous" people. Certainly there is no indication in early Jewish literature of that satirical perspective which both Greeks and Romans could employ in looking at the world. (Although in Plato too may be found the notion that humor, having a tendency to degrade art, religion and morals, should be avoided by civilized men [48]). It was of course a culture of piety, a theocratic society, that produced the Bible and the Talmud, and if humor is a way to breach the conceptual or cognitive framework then humor may be viewed as endangering the necessary wholeness of such a socially constructed framework. Besides, religion is itself a means of transcending at least the secular aspects of a given "social reality" and thus, if the religion is pervasive enough, makes another means of transcendence, such as humor, well nigh superfluous. But thinking along these lines merely suggests that where piety dominates, humor is not likely to thrive. One could, however, go further and say that the Jewish persistence in a religious social orientation, long after more this-worldly preoccupations had spread among their neighbors, indicates a group temperament inclined to a particular kind of "idealistic" and perhaps rigid frame of mind. It is not the kind of temperament associated with that looseness and flexibility inherent in satirical perspective.

It would of course be wrong to speak of "group temperament" as if it existed *sui generis,* coming from somewhere within, as it were. Such temperament must necessarily be connected with the variables of historical circumstance in which a national group is located. And so the early Jewish persistence in piety might be related, among other factors, to an austere economy, a severe climate, an embattled relationship with neighbors. A life of piety was a way to withstand adversity, even as it served to unify the people in their confrontation of it. Humor is of course also a way of subjectively warding off troubles but, as Salcia Landmann points out in the introduction to her collection of Jewish jokes (60), only if one begins to question one's cause or admits the possibility of defeat. Neither was the case, she suggests, with the Prophets, for example, who were uncompromising in their humorlessness precisely to the extent that they were uncompromising in their belief in the inevitable victory of Good over Evil.

It would be going too far, however, to flatly ascribe humorlessness, let alone a primitive incapacity to articulate amusement, to the early Jews. The generally serious bent of the literature cannot be justly interpreted as reflecting the *total* life panorama, and, in any case, the literature is in fact not devoid of descriptions of people being amused as well as "satirical." Thus, there is in Genesis an example of amused reaction to divine intervention in human affairs. The passage deals with a visit that three angels, disguised as men, are paying Abraham.

> And they said unto him. Where is Sarah, thy wife? And he said, behold, in the tent. And he said, I will certainly return unto thee at this time next year: and lo, Sarah thy wife shall have a son. And Sarah heard it at the door of the tent, which was behind him. Now Abraham and Sarah were old and well stricken in years: it had ceased to be with Sarah after the manner of women. Therefore Sarah laughed within herself, saying, After I am become old shall I have pleasure, my lord also being old. And the Lord said unto Abraham, Wherefore did Sarah laugh, . . . Then Sarah denied, saying, I laughed not; for she was afraid. [Gen. 18:9.] [Sarah later gives birth to a son] . . . And Sarah said, God hath made me laugh, whoever heareth it will laugh concerning me.
>
> (Gen. 21:6)

The name given to this son is Isaac, which means "He shall laugh."

For a biblical example of mordant irony rather than just amusement one might cite the passage in which the brothers of Joseph, jealous of his dreams of glory, conspire to kill him as he approaches them in the open field. "And they said one to another, Behold, here comes the dream master. And now, come and let us slay him. . . . And we shall see what will become of his dreams" (Gen. 37:19 quoted in 12). It must be kept in mind, however, that the irony is put into the mouths of "characters," in the context of the story *villainous* characters. The Bible's own voice remains unamused and non-ironical.

One can, however, even go further than this and adduce evidence that an "underground" current of attitude not at all in keeping with the Scriptures' sobriety existed among the people, as a passage such as the following from

Psalm 1 would indicate: "Happy is the man who walketh not in the council of the wicked, and standeth not in the way of sinners, and sitteth not in the company of jokesters." Satire, it seems, must have figured significantly alongside other iniquities. The point to be made, nevertheless, is that the dominant cultural orientation of the ancient Jews was a rigorously pious and anti-satirical one. They were accordingly not known among other peoples as having a capacity for a humorous interpretation of the world. Greeks and Romans could write facetiously concerning the Jewish intransigent "seriousness" in adhering to an austere monotheistic cult, whose symbol-shunning practices seemed outrageous to a polytheistic world studded with visible deities. But that Jewish seriousness only hardened in the face of the mockery.

Still, humor in *defense* of that seriousness was acceptable among Jews. A story told by the historian Flavius Josephus is similar in flavor to many another quoted in the Talmud. The story concerns a Jewish soldier named Massolamus taking part, among "an escort of Jewish cavalry," in one of Alexander's campaigns. During a march towards the Red Sea, the column was halted by the "seer" who was observing a bird and trying to determine, according to the bird's movements, whether the column should stay put, advance, or retreat. Upon learning of the seer's intent, "the Jew, without saying a word, drew his bow, shot and struck the bird, and killed it. The seer and some others were indignant, and heaped curses upon him. 'Why so mad, you poor wretches?' he retorted; and then, taking the bird in his hands, continued, 'Pray, how could any sound information about our march be given by this creature, which could not provide for its own safety? Had it been gifted with divination, it would not have come to this spot, for fear of being killed by an arrow of Massolamus the Jew'" (80, p. 18).

This kind of iconoclastic *chutzpah* humor is often found in the Talmud. One example is in the story of Abraham, who, as a young boy, secretly smashes every one of his father's idols except one, in whose hand he places a stick. When the father asks who did it, Abraham says it was the idol with the stick in his hands. The father says "But these gods can't *do* anything!" and Abraham says "Let your ears hear what your mouth is saying." Similar "cleverness" is frequently attributed in the Talmud to Jewish scholars in disputes of a theological nature. Thus, the Emperor Hadrian is said to have insisted to Rabbi Joshua that he wants to be *shown* the Jewish God. "Rabbi Joshua thereupon led Hadrian onto a balcony, saying 'Let us first look at some of His deputies.' The sun shining fiercely into their faces, Hadrian covered his eyes. 'I can't face it,' he said. 'Now imagine,' Joshua said, 'what would happen if you had to face God.'" (65)

There is a multitude of moralistic edifying stories, proverbs, puzzles, animal fables of a humorous cast in the Talmud, as well as simply droll or "marvelous" tales, such as those concerning Rabba Bar Bar Chana, a Talmudic Munchhausen, who tells, for example, of alighting on an island and settling down to light a fire and eat a meal when the ground beneath him begins to move and the "island" is revealed as the back of a huge fish (49). Yet humor of a critical, satirical kind is used, if at all, only in order to oppose foreign ideas; it is only turned outward. And there is in fact an explicit Talmudic dictum concerning the matter: "Rabbi Nachman said, All joking is prohibited,

except for jokes about idol worship" (Sanhedrin, p. 63).
In this historical period, then, the Jew—at least "officially,"
—does not yet laugh at himself.

Turning to later antiquity and the Middle Ages, one finds that here too piety persisted and with it the shunning of the kind of levity, or antagonism, associated with the satirical point of view. Formally, a break in public piety was sanctioned only once a year, in honor of the Purim festival. During that time it was customary to engage in irreverence; it was permissible, if not mandatory, to become drunk. The Purim gayety found creative expression in the *Purim-Spiel,* a farcical reenactment of the story of Purim, concerning the foiling of a plot against the Jews of Persia, performed by peripatetic amateur players. It was also on Purim that religious authority itself, as embodied in the rabbi, became subject to institutionalized persiflage: a town wag was appointed "Purim rabbi"; his function was to deliver parodies of sermons and pronounce ludicrous "decisions."

With the Talmud persisting as the very essence of Jewish cultural life through the middle ages and beyond, its tales and legends remained part of Jews' folklore, which was however enlarged by accretions borrowed and "naturalized" from the European reservoir of stories about the pranks of buffoons or the stupidities of simpletons. Other themes in the growing repertoire were the Jew in religious repartee with the Christian and the shrewd rabbinical pronouncement or judgment. However, as Landmann asserts (60, p. 40), the funny stories current among pre-Emancipation Jews cannot be considered what would today be called Jewish jokes.

It seems appropriate here to give some representative examples of that pre-Emancipation humor. The most famous figure in Jewish prankster stories, for example, is Hershele Ostropoler. Reminiscent of the much earlier Till Eulenspiegal, Ostropoler was an actual person who lived, in the 18th century, as an impecunious kind of court jester to Rabbi Baruch of Miedziborz (southern Russia). The Rabbi was afflicted with chronic melancholy and, perhaps as a consequence, promulgated the principle "It is sinful to be sad."

The following (next to practical jokes) are typical stories concerning Hershele Ostropoler (as quoted in 13):

His wife quarrels with him and says, "Who else would have married an ugly man like you?" H: "But I was really a beautiful child. Is it my fault that some witch exchanged me for an ugly one?"

H. drank a lot and was reprimanded by the rabbi. He explained: "Look, whenever I take a drink I become another person. And doesn't that person also deserve a drink?"

Someone asked H. why a coffin stands on two legs and a wedding canopy on four. H.: "In a coffin one person is buried, under a canopy two are buried."

H.'s wife has diarrhea. He runs to the rabbi who promises that he will recite Psalms for her recovery. Some time later she suffers from constipation and H. again goes to the rabbi, who again says he will recite Psalms. H.: "No, rabbi, don't you think those Psalms brought *on* the constipation?"

H., while traveling, doesn't doff his cap before a Polish noble. Pole: "Where are you from, Jew?" H.: "Ostropol." Pole: "And the cap?" (Formula used by nobles who expected Jews to remove their hats in their presence.) H.: "Also from Ostropol."

What is implicit in all these stories is the acceptance

by H. of the world in which he lives. This reflects the attitude of the Jew of that time who waited patiently for God to fulfill his purpose in the world. The irony of H. is directed not against the society in which he lives, nor against the oppressive outside society surrounding it, but against the very impulse to be dissatisfied or rebellious. The very ability *not* to contend against fate or society is exalted here into a kind of heroism. The reply to the noble is mildly audacious but one can imagine that H. at the same time removed the cap. And just as there is no aggressiveness vis-à-vis the Pole, there is none vis-à-vis the self, as expressed in the culture. The reply to the rabbi sounds impudent but hardly sacrilegious, as does a more modern version of that story in which the last line is "Oh, do Psalms work for constipation also?" Here the crass equation of the Psalms with patent medicine is that of a "modern" scoffing at religion; there the joke is perhaps primarily the unpredictability of the wife's digestion.

The classic Jewish simpleton stories are about the inhabitants of Chelm, a semi-mythical Polish Jewish town:

> The question was asked in Chelm which is more important, the sun or the moon. After long collective deliberation it was decided that it is the moon, since it shines at night, when it is needed, while the sun shines in the day, when it isn't.

A Chelmer walked in the rain with an umbrella that he didn't open.

"Why don't you open the umbrella?"
"It's full of holes."
"Then why did you bring it?"
"I didn't think it would rain."

One morning Chelm was covered with snow. It was decided that the *shamus* (beadle) should not make his customary morning round, calling people to prayer, because he would ruin the smooth whiteness. Instead, three men carried him. (7)

These stories, again, take the Jewish world for granted. The simple-mindedness caricatured is that resulting in awkwardness opposite nature itself. The narrator's implied competence in that area already justifies a sense of mastery. The world is as simple as nature, the stories say, and it takes little to be "at home" in it. The social situation, the personal identity are as unassailable as the sun, or the moon, or the snow.

This acceptance, reflecting a favorable self-image and a hope of final vindication and triumph in a Messianic age, was supported, and ultimately derived from, a strong ideological legitimation. Thus, in stories of encounters with Gentiles, the Jew comes out on top:

Priest (to rabbi refusing food because of dietary laws): "When will you finally discard these prejudices?"

Rabbi: "At your wedding, excellency." (56)

Big cities, to which Jews are beginning to move, are scorned:

Rabbi Hirsch Levin called Berlin a city full of piety. When people were surprised he explained that since everyone who goes there loses his piety, Berlin must be full of it. (56)

Among the Chassidic rabbis, the humor was focused affectionately on people's "little" failings:

Once several men talked idly during prayer in the presence of Rabbi Moshe Leib of Sassow. "Look, Lord of the Universe," he exclaimed, "even during their important discussions they invoke your name." (15)

But there is also a more anarchic strain in Chassidic humor:

When Rabbi Levi Jitzchak came to the prayer on Yom Kippur whose refrain is "He [God] said, I have forgiven," he interrupted the congregation and exclaimed, "Lord, we have no more strength to say '*He* said'—Lord, you yourself say it, say it yourself: I have forgiven." (15)

There is a sense of impatience here with old forms, yet its consequence is not a moving away but a deeper penetration of tradition. It takes a direction to be reversed only by later generations. In summing up the pre-Emancipation period, one might say that while there was Jewish humor, there was not what came to be represented later by the "Jewish joke": a radical self-questioning arising out of the appearance of the problem of Jewish identity.

THE HUMOR OF EMANCIPATION

IT WAS SUGGESTED ABOVE THAT THE JEWS WERE NOT A notably "humorous" people before the Emancipation period. This does not mean that they were not the *object* of humor on the part of others. Yet this kind of laughter, found in Christian satirical attacks down the centuries, probably did not "rub off," in the sense of engendering Jewish self-irony. This kind of laughter, often a prelude to murder, is not directly addressed to its victims; its effect is primarily to enhance the rage of those who laugh rather than to undermine the self-confidence of those laughed at. One might go further and say that these attacks, in their very outrageousness, must have served to confirm to the medieval Jew, firmly lodged in his Community of the Pious, both the extent of Christian ferocity and that of his own "righteousness."

With the beginning of Emancipation, however, a new kind of Jewish consciousness arose, which fed on the ambiguity implicit in the changed historical situation. Emancipation began in Germany, in the second half of the 18th century, with the convergence of what are in the beginning no more than two historical rivulets: the movement of "privileged" Jewish families from ghetto into town, and the movement of small German groups in the direction of the French Enlightenment. As these intellectuals, imbued with the new humanist-rationalist notions, began to turn to Jews in the attempt to test a freshly acquired, enlightened sympathy for *all* people, these Jews, in turn, were drawn to those ideas that brought them the exciting new experience of friendly social contact with, and acceptance by, their former oppressors. This convergence first took place in Berlin, where a number of rich Jewish merchants had been allowed to settle and where there was a certain amount of intellectual ferment, spurred by the interest of Frederick the Great in French culture.

The central figure at this meeting of two worlds was Moses Mendelssohn, whose own personality, in its transformation from Talmudic ghetto scholar to German philosopher, exemplified the rapid transformation that German Jewish consciousness itself underwent once that contact with the "world" had occurred. In 1742, Mendelssohn, in his teens, had made his way to Berlin from Dessau to follow his teacher in Talmud, who had assumed a rabbinical post there; but once in Berlin Mendelssohn had also begun to study mathematics and philosophy and to learn to speak German (when in the ghetto he had only spoken Yiddish). Over a game of chess he had made the acquaintance of the German poet Lessing, who was so impressed by this intellectually curious Jew that he became his devoted friend and introduced him to the foremost intellectual circles of Berlin. Mendelssohn absorbed and adopted the ideas of the Enlightenment, yet also maintained his devotion to Judaism. His intellectual goal was a kind of symbiosis of the two, a rational, deistic kind of Judaism. His book *Phaidon,* defending the immortality of the soul and advocating deistic religion, had an immense appeal both to German and Jewish readers in the

Enlightenment camp and beyond. Mendelssohn was hailed by many as the philosopher of the age.

In a memoir of Henriette Herz, who was one of a number of (eventually baptized) Jewesses of the generation following Mendelssohn's who became famous for their Berlin salons, which were for several decades the centers of German intellectual life, there is a revealing passage concerning Mendelssohn's remarkable social as well as intellectual talents:

> Of only one scholar in Berlin could it be affirmed that he had a home, if in one's definition of the word one includes the dispensing of hospitality to friends and acquaintances, even if uninvited. By profession this one and only scholar was a member of the commercial classes. His name was Moses Mendelssohn. In spite of his meagre earnings as a silk merchant's manager, scantily supplemented by the proceeds of his writings, and the six children for whom he had to provide, this admirable man kept open house: Foreign scholars seldom visited Berlin without getting someone to take them to him. His and his family's friends came without invitation, hence his daughter's brilliant female friends. Orthodox old Jews, to whom Mendelssohn always acted as a friendly coreligionist, came along too, but they were the most intellectual in the city . . .
> (14, p. 122)

The extent of the cultural gap bridged by Mendelssohn's career is illuminated by the memoirs of yet another immigrant to Berlin, Salomon Maimon, who later became a Kantian philosopher. In 1779, then a Talmud student on his way from Lithuania with the intention of studying medicine, he encountered in Koenigsberg (East Prussia) some Jewish medical students:

> These young men broke into laughter as soon as I appeared and explained what my plans were. Which is not surprising,

if one imagines a Polish-Lithuanian man of about 25 with a rather heavy beard, in torn and dirty clothing, whose language was made up of Hebrew, Yiddish, Polish and Russian, each with its respective grammatical errors. This figure claimed to know German and to have some knowledge of science. . . . They began to have fun with me and gave me Mendelssohn's *Phaidon,* which happened to be on the table, to read. I read miserably, and they broke into renewed laughter, asking me to explicate what I was reading. I tried to do this, but since they did not understand me they asked me to translate what I had read into Hebrew. I did this on the spot. The students, who understood Hebrew well, were not a little surprised when they saw that I not only understood this famous author but translated him into Hebrew with some felicity. They began to interest themselves in me then . . .

(8, p. 75)

Here the embarrassments and ironies of ambiguous identity are already very much in evidence. True, Maimon attempted an even more difficult transformation than Mendelssohn, coming as he did from the East European Jewish milieu which was so much farther still, in more than just the geographical sense, from secular Germany than Mendelssohn's German ghetto of Dessau. And Maimon indeed could not *bridge* the two realms; eventually, he jumped the gap, leaving Judaism behind forever. In fact the pattern of honorable symbiosis established by Mendelssohn hardly held good for anyone but himself. There was not only the intellectual distance between Judaism and "scientific" secularism, a distance that did not, as suggested, seem to Mendelssohn to make reconciliation impossible; there was also the nature of the two human groups involved. Here Mendelssohn erred in taking the few enlightened Germans he encountered as typical of Germans generally, and he also erred in taking himself, with his steadfast loyalty to Judaism and yet ready willingness to drop its "fossilized" peripheral phenomena, as typical of all Jews. Actually, only a small intellectual elite among the Germans had taken to the Enlightenment, and as for the Jews, they were generally either not willing to part with even the most minute aspect of tradition, or, if they had moved out of the ghetto, were most often tempted to discard even the "core" that Mendelssohn thought indispensable.

The latter tendency expressed itself in a movement toward conversion, which came in response to the prevailing German attitude regarding the conditions of Emancipation: the Jew could only gain full rights if he became a *true* German. If equality was to be dispensed to them, the old, medieval status of the Jews as a separate "nation" could no longer be tolerated. Napoleon's guideline became that of the Germans: *"Il faut tout refuser aux Juifs comme nation, il faut tout leur accorder comme individus."** But it was Judaism that defined Jewish nationhood, just as being a true German also meant being a Christian. And so Christianity became the destination of an important segment of the new Jewish Germans, including Mendelssohn's own children, initially beguiled though they had been by a new freedom emanating from a non-Christian, or even anti-Christian, Enlightenment.

By the early nineteenth century the German Jews, first to enter the history of the modern world, had become split into numerous camps of diverse tendency, and the scene was set for a collective sense of ambiguity, affecting all of them in different ways. As the gates of the ghettos opened, the variety of options open to the Jew also implied a variety of inherent taunts: the Jew who remains

---

* "Everything must be refused the Jews as a nation, but everything must be given them as individuals."

faithful to the old ways is a backward ignoramus, criminally scorning the benefits of German civilization; or, the Jew who converts is a renegade, an opportunist, a hypocrite, a coward; or, the Jew who "liberalizes" his Judaism distorts and emasculates it, ending up neither authentic Jew nor authentic German; or, the Jew who becomes *konfessionslos* (without confession) defrauds others and deludes himself, being still a Jew to the Germans and only a bad Jew to the Jews. And overarching this web of negative self-appraisals was the old, undiminished antagonism of the Germans, which found nourishment in the entire gamut of Jewish types, from the archaically garbed, exotically "sinister" traditional Jew to the church-going Semitic bourgeois.

At this juncture, then, no longer one of mortal danger for the Jews, or even of undisguised oppression, but suffused with the tensions of a multiple ambiguity concerning one's own ultimate worth and situation in life, a well-nigh all-pervasive irony invaded the German Jewish style of thought and discourse. A man must laugh, it seems, if he is to live with apparently insuperable incongruity in his life; and thus it was not surprising that the most important literary figure to emerge from among the Jews of Germany in that period was a poet, Heinrich Heine, whose work is stamped on nearly every page with that irony. There was, incidentally, an apparent escape route out of that ambiguity: socialism. Whatever the conscious motives of the predominantly Jewish founders of German socialism, its program certainly contained provision for the disappearance of Germans as Germans and of Jews as Jews within a kind of supra-national and supra-religious commonwealth. Yet socialism, whose "seriousness" is personified in the severe countenance of a Karl Marx, was chosen by only a comparative few. The rest, as industry and commerce expanded, became part of the new, ambiguously placed Jewish middle-class, taking the good of a growing access to trade, finance, and the professions, with the bad of a mutilated consciousness. But if Germany in the early nineteenth century may be safely given as the time and place of birth of modern Jewish Humor, it should be added that its antecedants included the centuries-old German tradition of anti-Jewish mockery, as well as an inbred Jewish capacity for subtle, paradoxical, dialectical patterns of thought, derived from the Talmudic style of logic as well as from an age-old need to live by one's wits.

The prototypical as well as outstanding figure of this Zeitgeist was Heinrich Heine. Born in 1796 in Dusseldorf, he experienced the entire spectrum of possible answers to the problem of Jewish identity then opening up. He was brought up in traditional orthodox Judaism; later he in turn experimented with "enlightened" Judaism, became fascinated by German Romantic nationalism, became converted to Christianity, turned to liberalism and Saint-Simonism, flirted with socialism, and, finally "rediscovered" Judaism. But more significant in what it indicates about the collective frame of mind of the Jews is the evidence strewn through Heine's writings that the diverse attitudes behind those consecutive life stages often acted upon him simultaneously, producing that tension whose result is irony.

Perhaps the best-known of Heine's *mots* is the one about the baptismal certificate being "the passport for entry into European culture." He cynically said this when already a "Protestant," having become baptized indeed with the motive of making an academic career possible and, paradoxically, just at a period when "his Jewish consciousness had reached a high-tide" (14, p. 250). This undisguised cynicism toward his Christianity must have proved soothing to his guilt feelings, as must have his castigation of other Jews who seemed to want to become "genuine" Christians. Yet he had previously, still officially a Jew, undergone a phase of Christian Madonna worship, seeking to replace an earthly madonna who had failed to love him with the heavenly one. On the other hand, he shortly thereafter joined a "Society for Culture and Science" whose aim was "to combine historic Judaism with modern science" (*ibid.*, p. 146). But yet again, he was not comfortable with a "rational," deistic Judaism, writing that "a few chiropodists have sought to heal Judaism of its putrescent skin troubles by blood letting, and as a result of their clumsiness and their cobweb rationalistic bandages Israel has to bleed to death. . . . We no longer have the strength to wear a beard, to fast . . ." (*ibid.*, p. 159). And yet again, in the same letter, "I, too, haven't enough strength to wear a beard and to let them shout "Abie" at me, and to fast . . ."(*ibid.*).

It seems useful here to quote a passage from Heine that conveys the flavor of the "new humor," essentially the modern Jewish Humor, which Heine is credited with introducing into German literature. In this passage from his travel sketches the narrator encounters a member of the nobility:

> Mathilde's warning not to be put off by the man's nose was well founded, and he really came close to putting out one of my eyes with it. I don't want to say anything bad about that nose; on the contrary, it had the noblest of shapes and it surely justified my friend to give himself at least the title of Marquis. For one could clearly judge by that nose that he belonged to nobility, that he had de-

scended from an ancient international family with which even almighty God himself had once intermarried without fear of a misalliance. Since then, to be sure, this family has come down somewhat in the world so that, since Charlemagne, it has had to make ends meet by commerce in old pants and Hamburg lottery tickets; yet it has never lost its ancestral pride, or given up the hope of regaining its old estates, or at least of receiving adequate indemnification once its old Sovereign keeps his promise of restoration, a promise with which he has led them by the nose for two thousand years. Could it be that their noses have grown so long because of their having been led so long by the nose? Or are these long noses a kind of uniform whereby the God-king Jehova recognizes his old bodyguard, even if they have deserted? The Marquis Gumpelino was such a deserter, but he still wore his uniform . . ."

(46, p. 261)

Even in this short excerpt many of the strands of Jewish Humor are visible. There is the playful language as such, the "dialectical" style, the crass metaphors. Then there is the two-edged sword extended toward the Jews: on one side the adoption of anti-Semitic cadences in connection with the nose, on the other the resentment of assimilation, characterized here as desertion; there is an ambiguous mixture of irony and bitterness in the remark concerning that "ancient nobility" and God's failure to keep His promise. There is finally the sideswipe at Christianity in the reference to God's liaison with that family, which Christians do not even consider worthy of toleration.

Heine was the best-known but by no means the only Jewish writer to introduce that Jewish irony into German literature. A veritable army of Jewish writers, especially feuilletonists, humorists, reviewers, polemicists, appeared, giving evidence of the historically imposed Jewish sense of irony, and stamping that irony on the German mentality as well. There was, for instance, the journalist Moritz Saphir, arbiter of the Viennese theatre during several decades of the early nineteenth century; his ironic *aperçu* concerning his several religious conversions reflect an outlook similar to Heine's: "When I was a Jew God could see me but I couldn't see Him, when I became a Catholic I could see God but He couldn't see me, and now that I'm a Protestant He can't see me, and I can't see Him." There was Ludwig Boerne, who, together with Heine, is credited with "inventing" the German feuilleton, a kind of casual humorous monologue that became a fixture in the German press. (An anthology, *Klassiker des Feuilletons*, published in 1965 by Reclam, most widely distributed paperback name in Germany, leads off with a humorous essay by Boerne, followed by one by Heine. Among the 31 writers represented, 13 are Jewish.)

In 1856 the English writer George Eliot, in her essay on Heine, credits him with actually transforming the German language: "There can hardly be any wit more irresistible than Heine's. We may measure its force by the degree in which it has subdued the German language to its purposes, and made that language brilliant in spite of a long hereditary transmission of dullness" (23, p. 415). And by 1876, at least, the reputation not only of Heine but of Jewish Humor generally seems well established even in England: "In his wit and humor Heine was a true child of the Hebrew race. However original he may have been, he exhibited the character and peculiarities of Hebrew humor, of the wittiest and most light-hearted people of the world, which, in the midst of unparalleled misfortunes and sufferings, has preserved an ineradicable buoyancy and an unconquerable spirit of satire." (*London Athenaeum,* January 15, 1876, quoted in 63, p. 83.)

The meaning or background of Jewish Humor may be imperfectly understood in these remarks, but the comic image of the Jews, in the very positive sense of comedy as a weapon against adversity, seems established. However, it is the image of the *German* Jews primarily that seems to be meant, whereas the bulk of the world's Jews was concentrated then in Eastern Europe. There, as will be seen, Jewish consciousness developed along somewhat different lines.

THE HUMOR OF NON-EMANCIPATION

IN EASTERN EUROPE, WHERE MOST OF THE WORLD'S JEWS lived at the end of the eighteenth century, the Enlightenment spirit, though it managed to penetrate that far, did not have the same consequences for the Jews that it had in Germany. To be sure, those notions of a new dawn for rational man, together with German romantic ideas of a rapprochement with nature, did provoke cultural impulses among some East European Jews similar to, or in imitation of, the first emancipatory stirrings among the Jews of Germany. Thus, Dubnow writes, "from Germany the free-minded 'Berliner,' the nickname applied to these 'new men,' was moving toward the borders of Russia. He arrayed himself in a short German coat, cut off his earlocks, shaved his beard, neglected the religious observances, spoke German or 'the language of the land,' and swore by the name of Moses Mendelssohn. The culture of which he was the banner-bearer was a rather shallow enlightenment, which affected exterior and form rather than mind and heart" (quoted in 102, p. 100). The new tendencies, here as in Germany, involved attempts at a redefinition of the meaning and practice of

Judaism. But the instrument for this effort, as was not to happen in Germany, was to be the Hebrew language itself, hitherto the bulwark of orthodoxy and reserved exclusively for prayer and religious scholarship. By beginning to publish Hebrew books and journals suffused with the new ideas, as well as providing textbooks of the sciences and translations of world classics in that language, the exponents of *Haskala* (which is Hebrew for "enlightenment") sought to bring about among the learned elite a gradual movement toward liberalized Judaism which, it was expected in conformance with the Enlightenment style of thought, would result in normalization of gentile-Jewish relations and the emergence of free and equal Jewish citizens. For a full life, the *Haskala* preached, such emancipation was indispensable and it was up to the Jew to achieve it through cultural self-purgation.

Indicative of how different the outcome of Jewish enlightenment was in Eastern Europe from that in Germany is the fact, for example, that the first secular Hebrew magazine, published in Germany in 1784, lasted only till 1794, since by then there were no longer any interested readers; they had all taken up the German language exclusively. In the East, however, the new, secular Hebrew literature was to grow in importance and last into the 20th century, when its domicile shifted finally to Palestine. Paradoxically, this apparent success is also indicative of failure. The masses of Jews in the East remained impervious to the lure of enlightenment, and thus this literature, its essentially missionary task perpetually unfulfilled, continued to have its ideological purpose, and therefore its *raison d'être*.

The reason for the difference between East and West was fundamental. In Germany a small Jewish population, numbering only 270,000 in 1820 (2), lived largely in city ghettos whose opening portals they only had to cross, exchanging their Yiddish for the similar German, as it were, in order to be in the German *Gesellschaft* (Society), if not *Gemeinschaft* (Community). Since expertise in trade and finance had developed among Jews for some centuries, their influx during the industrial upswing of the 19th century was not entirely unwelcome. Besides, there was the Enlightenment spirit to supply a rationale for this acceptance. In the East, however, there was neither the Jewish urge to integration engendered in Germany by physical and linguistic proximity to occasionally enlightened gentiles, nor were these nearly as positively motivated economically or ideologically. Millions of Jews lived in the East, i.e. Poland and the bordering areas of Russia, scattered primarily over numerous little towns and villages, in each of which they formed a separate and often numerically dominant, though oppressed, community, forming a kind of *lumpenbourgeoisie* of small shop keepers, artisans, porters, "agents," and idlers. Their most immediately visible gentile neighbors were generally peasants, the most "unenlightened" segment of the population. There was, to be sure, a government attempt, beginning with Nicholas I, at *enforced* Jewish "enlightenment" in the form of discouragement of traditional Jewish schooling and abolition of internal communal autonomy, yet these "benefits" came alongside continued harassments, such as abduction of Jewish children for eventual service in the Czar's army and baptism, or the levying of special taxes.

The Jewish masses, then, remained wary of emancipation, whether enforced by the Russians or advocated by fellow Jews via Hebrew literature. Yet that very refusal gave that literature, as has been suggested, a long lease on life, and allowed it to become institutionalized. And it is at this point also that one first encounters an *institutionalized* Jewish Humor, since "satire is the mark of *Haskala* fiction." (44, p. 52) It is in this aspect of institutionalization that the most significant distinction lies between the Eastern Jewish humor and that of the West. The latter grew out of a period of flux, if not chaos, and it was really the consequence of the individual's personal sense of ambiguity in being caught between two worlds. Its mode was self-expression, its purpose the inner relief from social tension (as well as the mining of that tension for commercially exploitable humor). The individual writer in the *Haskala* may also have felt the need for release from interior conflict, but his ultimate purpose was *preachment* to the masses. Certainly the very use of the Hebrew language limited the *commercial* potential, even as it added to the intended moral impact of the message. It was a message aimed of course exclusively at fellow Jews, and the function of the satire was not to afford the reader an easy laugh, but to arouse him to a serious reappraisal of his way of life. This was the first time in Jewish history that books appeared, written in the sacred tongue itself, which openly criticized and attacked the structure of Jewish belief and customs as well as the authorities embodying it. Yet these books were written, mistakenly or not, *on behalf* of Jewry. "The goal of early Hebrew literature was the realization of the new Jew, who would be humanistically expanded yet would retain his own colorful historical identity." (44, p. 54)

Among the subjects touched upon by the new, slightly heretical jokes now entering circulation alongside such harmless types as the Rothschild jokes, Landmann mentions the belief in miracles, the hope for the Messiah, the methods of Talmudic interpretation, the meaning of biblical texts, the faith in a world to come. As Irving Kristol points out, there arose a humor of "pious blasphemy" (58). In innumerable jokes, for instance, the form is that of edifying rabbinic discourse, while the content is impudent and sophistical. The following is a parody of Talmudic logic, to be sung in the prefigured melody of Talmudic study: "If I have the right to take money out of my pocket, from which the other man has no right to take money, then is not my right all the greater to take money from *his* pocket, from which even he has the right to take money?" "The form," according to Kristol, "is impeccably orthodox; only the content negates the purpose of this form, which in the Talmud aims at establishing the immutable principles of justice and piety" (*ibid.*). One might contrast this kind of incongruity of content and form with that employed by Heine when he parodies Schiller's *Ode To Joy* by writing: "*Scholet, holde Goetterspeise, Tochter aus Elysium . . .*"*; he substitutes *scholet,* a traditional Jewish Sabbath dish, for the original *freude* (joy). Here there is non-Jewish form with Jewish content, rather than vice versa.

Heine was certainly more familiar with the forms of German poetry than with those of Talmudic rhetoric and he played with the form he knew best. The butt of this joke, though, is still the Jew, even if it has none of that fierceness of criticism found in the eastern joke. Yet even that criticism apparently did not penetrate to the very core, since "almost no Hebrew author dared to ridicule the doctrines of the Jewish religion; it was only superstitions and trivial folkways that were frequently the

---

* "*Scholet,* lovely feast of the gods, Daughter of Elysium."

targets of attacks. Hebrew authors, even those of the *Haskala* period, had come to build rather than destroy" (44, p. 28). Thus the institutionalization of self-critical humor is accompanied, as it were, by the pronouncement "Let us improve things." The Jew is laughed at not because he is a Jew, but because he is not what a Jew really ought to be.

Yet there is often an intense bitterness in this Hebrew satire, as, for example, in the work of J. L. Gordon, who passionately attacked narrow rabbinical legalism. In one story a woman is forbidden by the rabbi ever to marry again after the bill of divorcement sent her from afar by her husband is found to contain an alleged misspelling of the husband's name. In another story a rabbi prohibits all the food and utensils a family has prepared for Passover when the wife reports having found a crumb of bread in the soup. The husband, who had wanted to keep the discovery a secret, is led by his wife's indiscretion to divorce her and is himself jailed by the Jewish (autonomous) community for attempting to keep a secret of such "gravity" (44).

Another Hebrew writer, Isaac Erter, attacked various established Jewish types: tax collectors, cantors, doctors, undertakers, mystics. Concerning a Chassidic "saint," Erter tells how the man's reputation originated: Once he has occasion to stay overnight in someone's house and he places a seed kernel on the body of a baby. The baby starts to howl, upsetting the whole family, who cannot quiet it. Finally the future "saint" secretly removes the kernel while pretending to "heal" the child. Abruptly the crying stops and the reputation of the "healer" is well on its way (91). And here is an undertaker speaking: "The dead I thought of as if they were fish caught in the net, to be turned into money; when a rich man dies I would think, Behold a Leviathan; and if a pauper died I would grunt, a crawling reptile is caught, a mere creeping thing" (*ibid.*). This undertaker is also so fanatical in his religious loyalties that he beats the corpses of men who do not have beards. Once he beats such a beardless corpse and suddenly the eyes open and the corpse rises. The undertaker dies on the spot.

Not surprisingly this literature was considered dangerous by many and it was prohibited among the pious. Yet the satire it produced reflected a portion of the general awareness. An ironic consciousness had in fact already begun to be fostered at an earlier period by the pious Chassidim themselves in their efforts to "loosen" the style in which Judaism was practiced. Not only did they shift emphasis from study as such to the telling of stories and the singing of songs, they agitated sometimes more demonstratively: "Abraham Kalischer was the leader of a group of Chassidim who were in the habit . . . of pouring scorn on the students of the Torah and the learned, inflicting all manner of ridicule and shame on them, turning somersaults in the streets and market places of Kolusk and Liozma and generally permitting themselves all sorts of pranks and practical jokes in public" (quoted from Dubnow, *Toldoth Hachassiduth* in 89, p. 334). The way for irony had thus already begun to be paved in the 18th century, when Chassidism appeared. The later newfangled jokes came to swim in the same stream bearing the Chassidic tales, and the message of the new Hebrew literature, even when it wasn't read, did not remain unknown. When satirists finally turned to Yiddish in the second half of the 19th century, the clamorous popular response to this ironic literature—now at last in the language of *all* the people—is evidence of an already well entrenched popular sense of self-irony.

The decision to turn to Yiddish was in itself not free from irony for the writers involved. Not only was it an admission that the earlier hopes of Hebrew literature for reforms "from the top," for a mass turnabout of the intellectual leadership, were pipe dreams, but Yiddish itself was considered a second-class language. Though universally spoken among the eastern Jews, it was used in print only for those stories, prayers, and renditions of the Bible intended for the superficially educated women and perhaps artisans. Thus, out of a sense of embarrassment, some of the subsequently most famous of Yiddish writers adopted at the start comic pseudonyms for their Yiddish (as distinct from their Hebrew) publications, as, for example, "Mendele, the Bookseller" or "Sholom Aleichem" (Peace unto you—i.e. How do you do). Yet Yiddish brought the mass audience, and although the large majority of Orthodox men remained as averse to the Yiddish as they had been to the Hebrew secularist literature, the Yiddish books often tended to reach their wives, and thus the men themselves.

At its beginning the Yiddish literature continued that sharp social and cultural criticism typical of the Hebrew writers, depicting satirically the ways of Eastern Jewish life. The first book by Mendele, for example, who was the first of the subsequently prestigious Yiddish writers, was "a devastating satire aimed at the corrupt politicians and hypocritical bigwigs who had risen to leadership in the Jewish communities and who were fattening on the spoils derived from taxes and religious imposts which these public benefactors were called upon (by the Russian authorities) to supervise" (concerning Mendele's *The*

Little Man, 63, p. 23). By the 1880s, however, the approach—especially as employed by Sholom Aleichem—had mellowed to a kind of shoulder-shrugging acceptance of the Jewish condition. The impulse of the earlier literature toward reform and self-emancipation lost most of its steam after the pogroms of 1881. And while a comparative handful of the young espoused socialist revolution, it was now realized even by the "enlighteners" that all attempts at moving in the direction of gentile society and culture were doomed to failure in any case, since it was evident that the gentile world was not ready to accept the Jews. At the same time, the decisive turn toward Zionist nationalism, or toward America, was yet to come. The possibility of a way out seemed suddenly remote, if not non-existent. But this mood becomes in Sholem Aleichem an untroubled self-affirmation, an approval of nearly all things Jewish, in effect a literature of consolation; he "loved his men and women for their weaknesses and their follies no less than for their quiet heroism and their mute idealism" (63, p. 174).

Thus the edge of high moral purpose, that essential seriousness of undertone, found in the preceding satirists, was blunted in Sholem Aleichem. For this was "that epoch when the greatest of all Jewish writers was—one can even say, had to be—a humorist" (58, p. 343). Not only had the goals of that earlier "serious" satire been proven illusory, but the life of piety also no longer could hold undisputed sway over thought and action. For a century the religious tradition had been undermined by the enlighteners and secularizers. Now fate could no longer be easily interpreted as an expression of God's sometimes fierce but comprehensible Will, subject to human influence through proper behavior. Moreover, Chassidism, by its emphasis on a more "familiar" approach to the deity, had contributed by this "humanization" of God to a greater sense of a world of inscrutable grace, rather than rational justice. The Messiah might still appear, but only God knew upon what provocation. This sense of divine unpredictability had been bolstered by the unpredictability of the Czar's government, which reverted to bloody oppression in the 80s after having for some decades shown some inclination toward liberalism. It is this disappointment in all hopes of the rational that Kristol sees reflected in Jewish jokes where rationalism is reduced to the absurd:

> Jew asks another to explain the secret of telegraphy.
> Second Jew: "Imagine a dog whose head is Kovno and whose tail is in Vilna. Pull the tail in Vilna and the bark will be heard in Kovno."
> First Jew: "But how does the wireless telegraph work?"
> Second Jew: "The same way, but without the dog."
> (58)

This sense of the irrationality of life, that despite poverty and oppression one could do nothing about it all vis-à-vis God or the Czar, brought with it an intimation of not being responsible for one's troubles. It must have been this kind of liberating notion that underlay the joyful humor of Sholom Aleichem and that must have infused the multitudes responding to it. Sholom Aleichem's comedy has the vitality of the totally powerless, of those who have nothing to lose. Being completely at the mercy of circumstances gives rise to a faith in "miracles," such as the one whereby Tevye, Sholom Aleichem's famous character, becomes a milkman: he picks up two prosperous ladies lost in the woods and is rewarded with a cow. In the following monologue he recalls his thoughts upon being brought by the two women to the *dacha,* where a fantastic array of food has just been laid out:

> I'm standing there, not too close, and thinking how, they should be preserved from the Evil Eye, how the rich of the town of Jehupets eat and drink. "Hock what you got, I say to myself, but be a rich man!" I'm thinking what falls off that table would be enough for my children for the whole week, till Sabbath. Dear God, sweet and faithful one, you are after all "Of Infinite Forbearance" [Hebrew quote], a great and good God, with mercy and justice, how is it you give to one everything and to the other nothing? One gets fancy pastry, the other plagues of the first-born? But then I think: you're a great fool, Tevye, what's the matter, you want to tell Him how to run the world? Obviously, if He decides it should be so, it has to be so; the best proof you have is if it had to be different it *would* be different. . . .
> (4, p. 29)

Another Sholom Aleichem character is Menachem Mendel, who appears in an exchange of letters with his wife (5). He has left his small town to go to Odessa and try his luck at "speculation." He thus puts himself into a setting where "miracles" are institutionalized. He is constantly on the brink of making a killing, but is doomed from the start to end up being staked by his wife for the trip home. He is the Jew who will never make it in the "modern world," but that world, the tone of the book constantly implies, isn't worth the trouble, while the wife who urges a quick sell-out and fast trip home is the salt of the earth.

There is in these letters a network of diverse comic contrasts, each representing an aspect of irony in the Jewish situation at that time and place. Thus, the very form of the letters: each one begins with a highly formal paragraph of address, in Hebrew, a standard one for the husband and another standard one for the wife. The wife's letters invariably begin: "In honor of my dear husband, the renowned leader, great scholar, the teacher of men Menachem Mendel, may his light shine." In the body of the letter, however, now Yiddish rather than Hebrew, she immediately commences to call him "fool," "idiot," "shlemiel." There is here a direct echo of that duality inherent in a *lumpenbourgeoisie* with grandiose historical memories and aspirations. But in addition to these oppositions of Hebrew and Yiddish, of third-person honorific and second-person insult, of the sacred and the profane, the content of the letters points up the contrasts between Russian and Yiddish, city and country, rich Jew and poor Jew, the old and the new.

Sholem Aleichem exploits the diverse nuances of bewilderment arising from these oppositions. There is, for example, a subtle distinction in the way the wife misunderstands the stock market and in the way the husband misunderstands it. When he writes home in glowing terms about the "golden business" one can do in Odessa and adds he is dealing in "London," which is "a kind of business where you can make your fortune in one day" (5, p. 12), she naturally answers in incomprehension: "Eighty black years on you. If you write already, can't you write like a *mensch*? Why don't you write out clearly what kind of merchandise that is in which you are dealing? Does it sell by the dozen? Or by the pound?" (*ibid.*, p. 14). In subsequent letters, Menachem Mendel's smug attempts to enlighten his wife about the stock market display his own total unawareness of what it all means: "As to what I wrote you about 'Transport,' this is, as I wrote you before, a kind of paper put out by a factory where they work on railroads and for which they give out 'divindend. [*sic*] The railroads are in Siberia, the papers are in Warsaw, and the customers are in Jehupets—Now you understand?" (*ibid.*, p. 63).

The comedy of Menachem Mendel is that, while he dreams of imminent glory, he doesn't have what it takes to become a success in the city. Yet there are enough Jews, as his letters show, that have become rich there. They must have left the small town with the same lack of knowledgeability concerning the world outside, as well as the same matter-of-factness about aspiring to become millionaires. For the "chosen" even the top-of-the-ladder holds no genuine surprise. Yet there was undeniable comedy in the spectacle of the oppressed provincial of yesterday becoming today's metropolitan big shot. And above all, the comedy of a problematic identity, one always beset by problems but never before fundamentally questioned, was to become the mark of the city Jew.

THE HUMOR OF THE CITIES

THE MOVE TO THE CITY MEANT ALSO, AS IT WERE, THE EXchange of Sholem Aleichem's world for that of Heinrich Heine. But this is essentially true only of those Jews from the east whose destination was a "Central European" city, usually a capital—Berlin, Prague, Vienna, Budapest. In these cities hovered that Heinean ambiguity that included even possibilities such as conversion to Christianity. Neither the Russian big cities themselves nor America offered quite the same climate: Russia remained too hostile and America was, in a sense, too hospitable. In America foreign cultural enclaves could be accommodated; it was in America that the Yiddish theatre had its most important development and Sholem Aleichem himself settled in New York, where he wrote his last Yiddish books.

America, of course, became the goal of most Jews leaving their homes in Eastern Europe at the start of the century. Not that Jewishness was to present no problems here. For one thing, the processes of Americanization triggered generational conflict, reflected in such popular Yiddish dramas as Gordin's *The Jewish King Lear*. Lincoln Steffens would write, after visits to the ghetto, of "an abyss of many generations; it was between parents out of the Middle Ages, sometimes out of the Old Testament hundreds of years B.C., and the children of the streets of New York today" (80, p. 291). The parents, however, had already demonstrated, at the very least, a less than total commitment to tradition by coming to America at all; one came with the thought of material betterment and with few illusions about the chances for a flourishing religious life. Those who valued the latter above all stayed home, no matter what the material conditions. Considerable time in fact elapsed between the start of the Jewish East European immigration and the arrival of the first rabbi of repute from those regions, and "moral leadership," according to Sanders (84), was first in the hands not of the religious but of the socialist intellectuals. Judaism, then, did not find the most favorable milieu in America, yet to be an "allrightnick" had to do with being a success in business, not with becoming a Protestant, or necessarily even with reading Walt Whitman. Becoming an American for the Jewish immigrant meant becoming an American Jew.

But if America did not demand apostasy, neither did it decree permanent quarantine. The Jewish "ghetto" of New York was felt to be a way-station rather than a terminal habitat. "The streets swarmed with Yiddish-speaking immigrants," writes David Levinsky, the hero-narrator of Abraham Cahan's novel of immigrant life. ". . . The scurry and hustle of the people were not merely overwhelmingly greater, both in volume and intensity, than in my native town. It was of another sort. The swing and step of the pedestrians, the voices and manner of the street peddlers, and a hundred and one other things seemed to testify to far more self-confidence and energy, to larger ambitions and wider scopes, than did the appearance of the crowds of my birthplace" (quoted from *The Rise of David Levinsky* in 84, p. 54).

However difficult it may have been, then, the new Jewish life in America was not "problematic" in the way it had been in Europe, and some of that more hopeful and innocent aura is conveyed in the traditional dialect humor of American vaudeville. Though it attempted to display "characteristics" of particular ethnic groups, the very basis of that humor was the fundamentally superficial attribute of mispronouncing the prevailing language. The essential implication was that if that person with the dialect were to make the correct noises he would soon be just like everybody else. And this implication was borne out by the "equalitarian" proliferation of dialects in vaudeville. Alongside the Yiddish dialect could be heard the dialects of the Scottish "Sandy MacPherrson" and the Swedish "Yohnny Yohnson," the Irish "Mick" and the Negro "Sambo," and sometimes the same comedian who "did" the Jew switched in turn to the "Dutchman" (German) and then to the Yankee. During World War I many of the Dutch comics converted to Yiddish dialect. The Jewish identity, then, tended to be no more "ticklish" a matter than that of other minorities. It became part of the American immigrant phenomenon.

The pattern of presenting the ethnic type in American vaudeville around 1900 is as follows: the particular type comes on stage dressed in the appropriate comic costume and does a song-and-dance proclaiming his identity and characteristics, according to prevailing cliché. The Scotchman sang of his frugality, the Irishman of his love of liquor, the Jew of his love of business. A very successful Jewish "act" of the time appeared "in a tall, rusty plug hat, long black coat, shabby pants, long beard which ran to a point, and large spectacles" (29, p. 288). His song went as follows:

> Oh, my name is Solomon Moses
> I'm a bully sheeny man,
> I always treat my customers the very best I can,
> I keep a clothing store way down on Baxter Street,
> Where you can get your clothing now I sell so awful cheap.
>
> Solomon, Solomon Moses,
> Hast du gesehn der clotheses?
> Hast du gesehn der kleine Kinder
> Und der sox is in der vinder? etc.

(Ibid.)

There is an innocence in this that is certainly far removed from Heine. And yet, by the beginning of this century, a "new humor" also began to make itself felt, a humor "more excited, more aggressive, and less sympathetic than that to which the middle classes of the nineteenth century had been accustomed" (66, p. 107). No doubt the new industrial urban climate must have contributed to this development, yet McLean, in his sociological study of vaudeville, points out that "the influence of German Jews was particularly strong in moulding the new humor" (*ibid.*, p. 114). It is however difficult to understand how it could be that the German Jews, who had been established in America for some time, suddenly had this direct influence, especially since that period was distinguished by a huge new influx of East-European Jews. More probably it was the Jewish humor *from* Germany, brought along by the immigrant Jews together with their own brand, that caused the upheaval. Edward Harrigan, turn-of-the-century playwright, probably came somewhat closer to the truth when he said "there's been a great change in the sense of humor in New York. . . . The great influx of Latins and Slavs—who always want to laugh not with you but at you—has brought about a different kind of humor. It isn't native, it isn't New York. It's Paris, or Vienna, or someplace" (quoted in 66, p. 106). Harrigan's geography seems somewhat uncertain, associating as it does Latins and Slavs with Paris or Vienna, but if he meant the East European Jews, as is most likely, then the association with Central European humor is not inappropriate. The Jews from the east had no doubt begun to absorb the modes of German Jewish humor into their own, even if essential differences between the two kinds of humor remained.

Probably the most important difference lay in the attitude to Jewish identity: it was only in the German Jewish humor that that identity itself came to be questioned. And it was in that humor also that the core lay hidden for the "ultimate" Comic Jewish Image, equating Jewishness with the comically absurd. As was mentioned above, such a questioning of identity was not naturally in the American air; the climate caused no group identity crisis. Yet that "new" humor, grown in the German climate and transplanted to Eastern Europe, was brought along with other European baggage, and it began to take root in America also.

To encounter that humor at first hand, one has to turn back to its natural German habitat, where the "naturally" ambiguous situation of the Jew manifested itself, among other things, in his eminence in comedy, satire, and social criticism. Some reference has already been made in a previous chapter (Humor of Emancipation) to humorous German Jewish writers of the 19th century, but in the

20th as well, or perhaps even more so, Jewish eminence in that field is evident. Thus, for example, the greatest satirist of Germany before Hitler was Kurt Tucholsky, and of Austria Karl Kraus; the most acclaimed German comedian Max Pallenberg; and to these Jews must be added countless other writers and actors who dominated the pre-1933 comic stage and film, the feuilleton, social polemic, and theatrical criticism. Moral concern and sometimes outrage was often present in the essentially satirical work of these men, which was addressed of course to issues at large and rarely directly to Jewish matters, though Jewishness lurked in the background. However, as one moves closer to "pure" entertainment, to show-biz, one begins to come across that style of comedy whose major ingredients include the very existence of the Jew, expressed in the Jewish Comic Image. The following anecdote, concerning the above-mentioned celebrated Max Pallenberg, taken from a 1924 joke anthology, might illustrate that style: Pallenberg was called to the telephone while playing cards with a group of friends. It turned out that the Marshal of the ex-King of Bulgaria was at the other end; he invited Pallenberg to dinner on behalf of his royal highness. Pallenberg was overwhelmed: "Yes, of course, I'll be very happy to come. . . . Oh, I eat anything, really, whatever you. . . . My favorite food? Oh, well, my favorite food is—er—" Here the friends shouted gleefully into the telephone, "*Matzos, Herr Marschall!*" (69). End of story.

Of course the comicality of Jewishness per se is probably still grounded here in the social situation of the Jew: the "shock value" of the word *Matzos* in the presence of nobility is contingent on the sub rosa pariah status of the Jew in society. He is funny, even, or especially, to himself because he somehow does not fit into the formal scheme of things. This lack of a sense of total at-homeness shows up in all the themes enumerated by Landmann (who is a European) in her typology of the modern Jewish joke. The following are some of these themes:

Business and banking: Jews had become closely associated with these occupations and their particular sins and foibles, the purchase of land or entry into craft guilds having been prohibited to them during the Middle Ages.

Hypochondria: The chronic precariousness of Jewish life in Europe, Landmann suggests, may well have exacerbated the Jewish sense of peril concerning real or imaginary sickness.

Kultur: When it became possible to do so, some Jews adopted western customs with such eager and solemn haste that they frequently fell flat on their faces.

Conversion: The converted Jew often felt it necessary to hide his origin, thus precipitating, among other things, the comedy of name-changing, and of the forced anti-Semitism of the converted.

Eroticism: The sexual restraints of the traditional Jewish world were mocked from the vantage point of the secular erotic freedom, but so was the looseness of that freedom.

Imaginary anti-Semitism: The Jewish habit of suspecting anti-Semitism even where it did not exist was a traumatically acquired social neurosis, so that mocking that habit constituted, as Landmann points out, not only self-criticism but criticism of society at large.

The joke collection referred to earlier (69), compiled by two Jewish comedians in Berlin, 1924, does not claim in its title to be a *Jewish* joke collection, yet the introduction points out that "the dominant joke, in life as in this collection, is the Jewish one" (*ibid.*, p. 4). The compilers facetiously indicate the well-established hegemony of this humor, stating that "in toto the editors were familiar with 45,657,387 jokes," the difficulty of choosing those to be included having been solved by submissions to the great grandmother of one of the compilers: "every one of those printed was laughed at by [her] as a brand new joke" (*ibid.*, p. 5). This collection manages to convey directly the Jewish mood and spirit of that time in Germany, and the following examples are typical and chosen at random:

> Plunder is raging in the streets during the 1918 revolution. A middle-aged Jew is among the looters. "For God's sake, Herr Rubin, you too, looting?" "Shhh, it's my own store."

> Pinkeles is in Shanghai, being pulled through the streets in a rickshaw. Suddenly the bottom falls out. The rickshaw boy is unaware of what has happened and keeps pulling. After a quarter hour Pinkeles knocks on the boy's shoulder: "Rickshaw man, I think I'm running."

> Business letter: Messrs. Ignaz Baum & Co., Berlin. You have had the temerity to send me an insolent demand for payment. I hereby advise you that all unpaid bills are put into a drawer of my desk. On New Year's day that drawer is opened, one invoice is pulled out at random and paid. If you should dare to send me another one of those demands for payment you shall be excluded from the lottery. Yours very truly, Arthur Porges.

> Pinkus meets Adler on a North Sea beach. Adler is carrying buckets: "I'm totally broke and have to carry sea water into the hotels for 10 pfennig a bucket." Next day Pinkus comes to the beach when the tide is out. He looks at the receded shore line: "Boy, must Adler have made money yesterday!"

The ultra-nationalist Representative from Hellwig has taught his parrot one phrase: "Ugly Jew!" He donates the bird to the zoo. The bird repeats the phrase just as Jonas Goldbaum, from Tarnopol, passes before the cage. Goldbaum: "With a nose like that, look who's talking!"

Little Max is telling his father about having studied centipedes in school. "That's an animal with a hundred feet," he explains. "But how can one tell if an animal has a hundred feet?" "Oh, a *goy* counted them."

Sternfeld to beach acquaintance: "I'm losing 1000 Mark every week in my business." "Why don't you close?" "And from what shall I live?"

A man appears in a business office. "Herr Tietz? I saw your ad in which you look for a young, educated, experienced man. I am 58, speak a little German but mostly through the nose, and have been a *shnorrer* all my life!" "Well, what are you doing *here?*" "I just wanted to tell you that the job is *not for me.*"

Mesritzer visits Pollack, who is sitting in his room naked, except for a top hat. Mesritzer: "Why are you naked?" Pollack: "Well, nobody comes here anyway." "But why the top hat?" "Maybe somebody does come."

Klinger: "I know you had that small car accident. How much did you get for that light injury?" Singer: "15,000 Mark." "That much?" "Well, when I saw it's hopeless I gave my wife a kick in the *ponim*" (face, in Yiddish).

"Do you prefer Christian or Jewish girls?" "Christian. When you kiss one she shouts 'Jesus! Mary!' but nobody comes. When you kiss a Jewish girl she shouts 'Papa! Mama!' They come."

Modern parent: "I allow my daughter to act in risque films, but I would never permit her to go and see them afterwards."

The Ten Commandments is being shown at the Grosses Schauspielhaus movie theatre in Berlin. There is dead silence in the audience as the long stream of the Children of Israel enters the Red Sea. Suddenly a voice from the audience: "Hey, isn't that Schlesinger over there?"

These jokes convey the fissures in the soul of the European Jew in modern times. There is impudence and timidity, haughtiness and servility, self-indulgence and self-disdain, savvy and helplessness in these jokes: the supposedly unimaginative *goy* is airily assigned the pedestrian task of counting a centipede's feet, yet there is hesitation in telling the rickshaw boy that the bottom has fallen out; the demanding job is proudly scorned by the *shnorrer*, yet one carries sea water in buckets; the new permissiveness is embraced (allowing one's daughter to act in sex films), yet the old morality is clung to (forbidding her to watch them); the Exodus is watched in awe, yet one only sees Schlesinger from next door; one wears a top hat, yet is naked. Perhaps that surrealist figure alone in a room, removed from the social world, already is the ultimate Jewish Comic Image. Herr Pollack, the Jew, has become funny *independent* of social circumstances.

Approaches to the Jewish Comic Image may be charted however not only in the German joke but in the media of that time, or at least the film, as well. For example, a whole series of comedies starring Ernst Lubitsch, who was later to become a famous film director, featured "Meyer" or "Moritz," archetypal German Jewish names, in a variety of comic settings. Thus, in 1913 Lubitsch had already appeared in *Meyer on the Alps*, a title echoing a popular song of the time *"Was macht der kleine Mayer auf dem grossen Himalaya?"* ("What's little Meyer doing on the big Himalaya?") (101, p. 297). Other comedies were *The Firm Gets Married* (1914) with Lubitsch as apprentice Moritz Abramowski, *Meyer Becomes a Soldier* (1914), *The Black Moritz* (1916), with Lubitsch in blackface, *Shoe Salon Pinkus* (1916), *Prince Sammy* (1918). From these titles alone it is of course clear that Jewishness as such, in whatever the circumstances, is already a highly marketable comic ingredient.

To return now to the United States during the first decades of the century, it is that ironic perspective of the Central European Jew that has by then invaded and partially transformed American comedy. Not only do typical American-Jewish jokes sound like the jokes of Europe quoted here, while American productions like *Potash and Perlmutter* recall the Lubitsch films, but that satiric point-of-view, if not its actual content, becomes domesticated in American comedy in general. One may point to the fact that Lubitsch himself was to introduce "sophisticated" comedy to Hollywood. Yet, as the preceding study of the media indicates, the explicit reference to the Jew was itself eventually to become, in its more "arbitrary" form, an important component of American comedy.

The road toward this culmination can be traced along the decades in the changing relationship between Jewish comedian and American comedy. The early "innocence" of the vaudeville Jew eventually gives way to the more recondite "European" ironies of Jewish comedians appearing before more exclusively Jewish audiences, at social gatherings, in mountain hotels, in New York nightclubs. At the same time, the Jewish comic impulse also erupts nationally in "stars" like Ed Wynn, Eddie Cantor, later Jack Benny, Danny Kaye, who speak to the broad American public in an ethnically "neutral" humor. Two strains of Jewish comedian thus become visible: the famous one, whose humor is not explicitly Jewish, and the obscure one, whose humor is. It is the latter, catering directly to the intense taste in Jewish audiences for that self-irony learned in Europe, who is to be the crucial figure in bringing explicit and arbitrary Jewishness to American comedy.

A brief consideration, necessarily speculative in part, of some of the "inner" as well as outer features of this "parochial" comedian's professional life reveals the mechanism that soon causes him to produce that arbitrary kind of humor, associated with the ultimate Jewish Comic Image. From financial and professional considerations it becomes necessary for the parochial comedian to extend his appearances to far-flung places such as, say, a night club in Kansas City. Now his entire comic *persona*, developed in front and for the sake of Jewish audiences, is of course Jewish, and it necessarily remains so even before the non-Jewish audience. But beyond this, a strong motivation arises for the comedian in the Kansas City situation to emphasize his group identity, to "push" it, since he discovers that the very shock of its strangeness creates laughter, especially if encouraged. What now happens is that, while the actual content of the humor must necessarily become less Jewish, since non-Jews are not likely to understand Jewish "in" jokes, the *fact* of Jewishness itself, much more taken for granted by the Jewish audiences, becomes an important component of the humor. Thus, a Yiddish phrase that was laughed at by the Jewish audience, especially in the early decades, because of its funny meaning, might be laughed at by the gentile audience because, though incomprehensible, it is Yiddish.

If the parochial comedian, at this stage, thus brings arbitrary Jewish humor before small gentile and eventually probably Jewish audiences, he moves onto the national scene with the advent of TV at the beginning of the fifties. TV requires large quantities of "talent" and the Jewish parochial comedian, already much more numerous than other parochial comedians, heeds the call. TV is hospitable to him, since the Jew (as the attitude surveys pertaining to this time suggest) is no longer considered "dynamite." And when the Jewish comedian faces the TV audience, he of course does what he has become accustomed to doing in the Kansas City nightclub: noting the laughter engendered in the audience by the shock of encountering the previously tabu Jew, he uses Jewishness itself as a comic prop. And so begins the institutionalization of the Jewish Comic Image in the American media.

THE HUMOR
OF THE ANTI-SEMITES

ANTI-SEMITIC HUMOR, LIKE THE HUMOR OF THE JEWISH Comic Image, is unconcerned with the actuality of Jewish life. But unlike that professionalized Jewish humor which uses the idea of the Jew as raw material, so to speak, in the process of producing laughter, anti-Semitic humor uses laughter to create that idea of the Jew which the anti-Semite wants to exist. While the causes for Jew hatred are complex, it is in the nature of anti-Jewish caricature to supply rather simple fantasies that can be used to support that hatred. Besides, the only Jew the gentile *can* fully imagine in these productions seems to be a projection of his own more unworthy self. One such fantasy would appear to be the *Judenschwein* ("Jew-sow") theme frequently encountered in the middle ages. Carved into the façade of the thirteenth century Regensburg cathedral, for example, this "Jew-sow" is shown as it is being milked by Jews in their cone-shaped Jewish head-gear (28, as all other examples, unless noted otherwise). In a print for a 1519 pamphlet the Jews are shown not only milking the sow and drinking from its teats, but one Jew lovingly holds a Hebrew script in front of the animal's face. This ubiquitous motif transforms the pig, the very symbol of all that is taboo for the Jew, into a veritable Jewish love-object. But this fondness for the pig is of course more typical of the gentile himself. In going "behind the scene" of Jewish life then, the gentile can only imagine *himself* in the shoes of the Jew. This projection mechanism operates in all anti-Semitic humor, since the vital "inner" side of the Jewish mentality must of course remain unknown to the non-Jew.

It is difficult to know whether that kind of fantasy is avowedly meant to be taken as just that, or whether a pretense of "reportage" is involved. Certainly the Hebrew-reading (or studying) pig would stretch credulity. One comes across other motifs where the renditions look more realistic: the drawings depicting Jews enjoying the blood of Christian infants suggest in their sobriety of style the medieval equivalent of a modern news-photo, picturing actual events. Obviously, such drawings were not intended to be funny at all. But even where laughter is the intended effect, and even where the subject matter is self-evident fantasy, as in a woodcut of 1517 showing Jews, garbed in cloaks marked with the obligatory yellow circles, but with animal faces and hoofs and claws, the intention is to produce a Jew that can be more easily hated, and, sometimes, killed.

The emphasis in the production of the hateful Jew through caricature moved toward an every-day realism by the 17th century. Outright fantasies of the medieval kind slowly gave way to the relatively minor adornments of reality compatible with the declining metaphysical cast of mind. One standard form taken by these more subtle reality adjustments was the Jewish Nose, which eventually became the simple and "realistic" device *par excellence* for the allusion to Jewish Evil. The major motif now became Jewish money lending, but already in the 17th century the Jew as such, even one not involved in nefarious or grotesque activity, was a comic object: a painting of a 17th-century Nuremberg Jew shows in careful detail a rather commonplace face of a middle-aged man, except for the slight exaggeration, not of his nose in this case, but of his curled, "oriental" lips. He is in the act of shouting, the caption being, *"Wai geschrien!"* the German-Yiddish for "Woe is me!"

The "realistic" approach is perhaps best exemplified by Rowlandson's 18th-century Jewish caricatures. The subjects are the Sephardic Jews who since Cromwell's time had begun to settle in England. As on the Continent, they were restricted to such occupations as money-lending and dealing in old clothes. Rowlandson's drawings range from low-down London street scenes of bearded old-clothes Jews, ragged, long-nosed, to the drawing room of the well-dressed banker Solomon, hook-nosed and bearded also, flanked by two bare-bosomed trollops gripping the bags of money he is holding. Caption: "Solomon delighting in two Christian beauties." Poverty and wealth are made equally sinister in these drawings through the common denominator of the Jewish Nose.

In 19th-century German and Austrian caricature, Emancipation and the resultant drift toward assimilation—coupled with upward mobility—became major subjects of mockery; the Jewish Nose now served as comic contrast to the newly adopted "western" clothes, manners, and attitudes. The place of the medieval Jewish ogre was taken by the awkward *shlemiel,* laughter now having become the *only* acceptable manner of relieving the tension of hatred. Yet, significantly, the *shlemiel* prototype, at least as introduced into German literature by Adelbert Chamisso (a non-Jew), in 1814, is guilty of dealing with the devil. Similarly, the *shlemiel* is shown in anti-Semitic humor to be crafty and shrewd, as well as awkward and inept: there is the totally inappropriate *look* of the big-nosed Jew in gentile guise, and there is the total concern with money and its conspicuous consumption. At the same time, the more traditional type of ghetto Jew continued to be caricatured as well, and it was in fact that older image which made possible the emphasis on incongruity in the portrayal of the Jewish *arriviste*. The Jewish Nose was thought of for so long in connection with the old-clothes man that it looked doubly absurd in the outfit of a Biedermaier fop.

In the early 1800s, moreover, the then fashionable Romanticism was exploited to heighten this humor. In a cartoon of 1820 an expensively elegant lady with Jewish Nose is seen gazing at the moon, but she is described as imagining that the moon is probably made of genuine silver. Another cartoon of that year simply shows a fashionably dressed couple, long-nosed, in affectionate mood. Caption: David and Bathsheba. Here there is no mention of a lust for money, yet the Jewish Nose presumably says it all. Other cartoons attacked that alleged interest in money more directly, in ways ranging from wry to farcical. Wry: A young wife is seen standing in back of her husband's chair, her face strained, while her husband is absorbed in examining jewelry through a lupe. Caption: The Exercise of Patience in Jewish Married Life (1825). Farcical: A family is seen gathered around a table on which a little boy is squatting over a pot, with bare behind. Caption: Little Israel has swallowed a ducat (1820). Often, however, the indictment is more severe. In a cartoon showing Jewish "speculators" in top hats standing near the entrance to the stock exchange, a little boy is stealthily pulling a handkerchief out of one man's pocket. Caption: "Herr Baron, the boy is stealing your handkerchief." "Leave him alone, we also started small" (1851).

Turning next to examples of anti-Jewish prose of the period, one again comes across the theme of the *nouveau riche* Jew. In a joke book published in Austria in 1827 (87), for example, there is a humorous prose sketch entitled *Israel's Jubilation or the Birthday of the Great Contractor*. It describes a sumptuous feast, arranged in honor of the fiftieth birthday of Abraham David Wallfisch by his son, Jean Pierre. Members of the nobility are among the guests, as it is Wallfisch's secret desire to acquire a title. Wallfisch enters the main drawing room "led on both arms by two winsome Israelite lads." A large portrait of Wallfisch shows him on a horse, in front of a wagon of army supplies, riding down a hill toward a group of weary soldiers "who stretch out their emaciated arms in his direction, shouting, 'Hosanna! Praised be he who cometh there!'" Also among the guests is little Jacob, the youngest son of Wallfisch. "Already as a suckling babe, resting at his mother's breast, he lusted after her ear-rings, and he removed one of them while she slept and hid it cleverly in the folds of his garment; for which deed the elders of Israel did praise him and prophesied that he would one day stand out in intelligence and wealth among all from the tribe of Grab." During the festivities, the older Wallfisch announces a gift of twenty Gulden for the local needy and little Jacob, "who had been busy forming little bread balls into ducats," shouts, 'Father! What are you doing?' Herr Wallfisch answers him with gentle wisdom: 'My son! When one gives to the unfortunate, one receives a hundredfold interest.' 'What!' answers little Jacob. 'Watch out, you will lose interest and capital too.' Upon this remark there arose laughter among the people and all Israel praised the lad's wisdom and spoke: 'Blessed are the breasts that gave suck unto such a son.'" The climax of the feast is an elaborate performance involving girl dancers impersonating the moral attributes. After the performance, Wallfisch is glimpsed whispering to "Virtue": "After midnight, as arranged." It might be noted that the piece employs the incongruous biblical rhetoric in the same way the caricatures employ the Jewish Nose: grotesqueness on the surface, with rumblings of the sinister underneath.

By the end of the 19th century, and probably much earlier, the Jew as *shlemiel*, as archetypal clown, with a glint of Evil—primarily economic Evil—in his eye, had become a standard protagonist of the ubiquitous Jewish joke in Central Europe. The two prime sources for these jokes were the anti-Semites and the Jews themselves, and while the latter might sometimes see that aspect of Evil as really a kind of lovable roguishness, it was in the end often difficult to distinguish the source of a joke. A glance at the examples, given in the previous chapter, of jokes published by Jewish compilers will indicate their similarity to anti-Semitic jokes such as the following taken from an Austrian collection published (under gentile auspices) in 1899. (75)

Rabbi: I want to borrow a hundred gulden.
Seifenstein: But Rabbi, you preached yesterday that one shouldn't lend money on interest, that it is worse than murder.

Rabbi: But I want the money without paying interest.
Seifenstein: Oh, but that's worst of all. That would be *suicide*.

Anschel: Is it true that Mundi Schelzer became converted?
Sandor: Yes, he told me himself.
Anschel: But why did he become a Catholic, of all things?
Sandor: He thinks there are already too many Jews among the Lutherans.

Servant: A lame beggar downstairs asked me if you're here. Shall I have him come up?
Banker Schneutztuch: Lame, you say? The poor man! Run down and tell him he shouldn't exert himself for nothing.

Two Jews pass a beautiful woman. One spits.
— Shloimy, why do you spit before such a beautiful woman?
— Ass, I don't spit before the beautiful woman. I spit because of that woman I have at home.

Two Jews on a sinking ship.
— Oi, the ship is sinking!
— What are you crying for? Is it yours?

A Polish Jew comes to Hungary and sees a sign next to a lake:
BATHING STRICTLY FORBIDDEN.
Polish Jew: Crazy Hungarians! Who thinks of bathing?

— Why are you still single?
— Well, whenever I'm about to fall in love the girl's family is never rich enough.

Teacher: How many legs does a June bug have?
Little Moritz: Teacher, you have any other problems?

Shloimy: Rivka, I made a hundred gulden today.
Rivka: How come, Shloimy?

Shloimy: Well, on my way to Bratislava somebody stopped me and took away my wallet. If there had been a hundred gulden inside I would have lost the money. Since I didn't, I have made a hundred gulden.
Rivka: Lueger (Anti-Semitic mayor of Vienna) should only live from such business.

David Eisenstein, cattle merchant from Papa (small Hungarian town), cables his wife: Because the 9 o'clock train does not take oxen, I am coming tomorrow.

Boss: Why did the customer leave without buying?
Salesman: The woman wanted blue stockings, which we don't carry.
Boss (in a rage): Idiot, why didn't you sell her a red flannel muffler?

The atmosphere of these jokes, unflattering as it is to the Jew, does not exclude the "lovability" of the clown. Such jokes, anti-Jewish though they are, were not unacceptable to the Jew himself, and he incorporated a great part of their snideness into his own jokes. But the 20th century brought back that Jewish ogre of the middle ages whom the *shlemiel* had for some time replaced. The strain of "subtlety," to be sure, was not exhausted. The Munich magazine *Simplicissimus,* for example, published a cartoon in 1907 showing some elegant types with moderately drawn Jewish Noses at a Nativity Play in Berlin. One elegant lady remarks: "I find the idea *so* original." Yet the thoroughly satanic Jew made his reappearance, especially in conjunction with the sharpening of ideological dissension. A German cartoon of 1905 entitled "Underground Russia" shows a tunnel being dug underneath Russia by fierce-looking Jewish radical types, while another, of 1900, shows a smug Jewish bourgeois family riding a car whose "engine" consists of hard-working "Aryan" laborers. And in a handbill issued by the *Deutschnationale Partei* in 1919 a row of caricatured Jewish faces, representing among others such politicians as Rathenau and Bernstein, is captioned "Your *present* leaders. Do you want different ones? Then vote *Deutschnationale!*" This leaflet was a precurser of the later Nazi cartoons where the Jewish Nose became apotheosized into the supreme symbol of Jewish Evil. In the 1919 leaflet, the undesirability of the leaders pictured is felt to be sufficiently established by nothing other than the particular configurations of those facial features. That Jewish Nose had become a literal Comic Jewish Image of Evil, with eventually deadly consequences.

Most of the cartoon examples in this chapter are German, not only because culled from a German anthology, but because Germany was the most fertile source of this humor, although Austria, Russia, France, and England also contributed. As for the United States, a short survey of the two important humor magazines in the late 19th and early 20th centuries, *Judge* and *Life*, shows the Jews as occasional butts between the years 1885 and 1925, together with the Irish, Negroes, and Chinese.

The issues of three months (September, October, November) for the years 1885, 1905, and 1925 were looked at to determine the impact of the vast immigration of East European Jews on American attitudes. The two magazines show contradictory tendencies. *Life* featured some anti-Jewish cartoons in the periods checked for 1885 and 1905, but none for 1925. The one cartoon for 1885 occurs in the September 17 issue. It shows a Jewish rag man, in long black coat and beard, weighing a sack on a hand scale in front of a housewife. Rag man: "Madame, shust dventy-four pounds." Biddy: "Ye old scoundrel, it weighs over 40, for Oi weighed it meself." Rag man: "B-lieve me, madame, I wouldn't sheat a child. But, my scales will only *vey* dventy-four bounds." The only cartoon for the 1905 period occurs in the October 4 issue. A man with Jewish Nose carves a human statue marked 'Drama,' resting on a pedestal marked 'Trust.' The caption says: "Soon to be numbered with the lost arts and lost tribes." Apparently, this was an attack on Jewish influence in the theatre. In the 1925 period, not a single cartoon of Jewish content was found.

Judge, on the other hand, yielded nothing in the 1885 period. In 1905 it featured a cartoon in which Teddy Roosevelt is shown in defiant stance, telling the Czar: "Stop your cruel oppression of the Jews." In the background an old Jew, with an immense burden on his back is leaving a burning town, followed by his family. This is the only cartoon of Jewish content for the 1905 period (Sept. 30). In the 1925 period, however, there are two. On September 14th: as part of a weekly series called *Seeing America Worst*, there is the drawing of a book. On one page, "You are now entering N.Y.C., N.Y." On the next page, a big Yiddish inscription. The other cartoon occurs in the October 12 issue. It is acknowledged to the *Princeton Tiger* and shows two Jews. "Say Abe, vat do you think of the idea of founding a New Jerusalem?" "Oi, it's foolishness, Ezekiel. Ain't we still got New York?"

Nowadays, of course, such cartoons, especially if *anti*-Jewish, are not likely to be encountered in the American (or German) press. Echoes of this humor do however reverberate today in the Jewish Comic Image, a creation of the Jew himself.

III

THE HUMOR OF THE JEWISH COMEDIAN

THE JEWISH COMEDIAN, PROFESSIONAL EXPONENT OF THE Jewish Comic Image, has become a cultural institution in American society. To be a Jewish Comedian is to conform to an established role vis-a-vis the public. The dominant behavior pattern of that role, as an ideal type, is sufficiently set to make it possible for anyone, even the non-Jew, to adopt it. Thus the example of gentiles in professional comedy who assume speech patterns, attitudes, jokes, and Yiddishisms belonging to the Jewish Comedian. In American comedy, the word *shtik* (for "comic bit") is used universally.

But not *all* comedy, of course, is now that of the Jewish Comedian. There are comedians purveying the "universal" comic point of view (or at least the broad "American" comic point of view), such as Bob Hope, Jackie Gleason, Jonathan Winters, and there are Jews—for example Jack Benny—among them. Their comedy does not bear any tag except that of humanity: they are *just* comedians, with no special group affiliations. Moreover, there are, of course, other subdivisions of humor besides the Jewish, such as Negro humor, yet the Negro as comedian is not so distinctive a cultural prototype, if one considers the more current public roles of the Negro as jazz musician, as boxer, as militant. Besides, Negro humor itself today often is a form of militancy (cf. chapter on television). The Jewish Comedian, however, competes against no other Jewish cultural prototype in the media. The Jew and comedy are officially married; if the Jew, as a Jew, has any role to play in the media, it is comedy, and if comedy has any *special* label, it is most often Jewish.

The situation manifests itself statistically. "Most comedians," according to Steve Allen, a non-Jewish television performer, "are Jewish." (6, p. 212) He enumerates: "Jack Benny, Groucho Marx, Red Buttons, Charlie Chaplin, Jerry Lester, Ed Wynn, George Burns, Morey Amsterdam, Henny Youngman, Jack E. Leonard, Milton Berle, Larry Storch, Danny Kaye, Jan Murray, Joey Adams, Phil Silvers, Robert Q. Lewis, Eddie Cantor, Jerry Lewis, Ritz Brothers, Arnold Stang, Henry Morgan, Parkyakarkis, Paul Winchell, Bert Lahr, Phil Foster, Myron Cohen, Ben Blue, Abe Burrows, Phil Baker, Irwin Corey, Sid Caesar, George Jessel, Dick Shawn, Fletcher Peck, Buddy Hackett, Shecky Green, Georgie Kaye, Alan King, Sam Levinson" (6, p. 213). To which list, compiled in 1956, may be added Woody Allen, Shelley Berman, Joey Bishop, Jackie Mason, London Lee, Rodney Dangerfield, Lennie Bruce, Mort Sahl, Don Rickles, Jack Carter, Sandy Baron, and many others seen on television.

The names listed are, or were, comedians who are Jewish, but not all, as has been suggested, fit the typology of the Jewish Comedian. This role model, which will be looked at more closely somewhat later, may be characterized as essentially opportunistic in its Jewishness: there is no involvement in Jewishness, yet every willingness to use it to its utmost as a comic prop. Some of the names listed by Allen, however, are in that older tradition of comedy arising directly out of the special, ambiguous Jewish situation and hence special perspective on the world. The Chaplin tramp, for example, explicitly Jewish in *The Great Dictator,* is really difficult to "place" into any other symbolic niche but that of the Jew in the Diaspora. His threadbare elegance and precarious dignity may convey a nondescript aristocrat come down in the world, but whence the amazing agility, the tendency to kick pomposity in the behind? The striving against all odds for the proper appearance, in black bowler, tight frockcoat, and striped pants, may suggest the dandy out of money, concerned about maintenance of *la bella figura,* yet does the tramp spend even a moment in front of the mirror, primping? Actually, his very fondness for women is so hearty and "natural" as to leave no room for narcissism. It would appear rather that his concern for correctness in dress is an expression (as it has been in Jewish tradition) of his generally "respectable"—in the sense of moral— orientation: he believes, amazingly enough, in comforting the innocent and helpless and in fighting, mocking, and outrunning the snobs and bullies. And that the latter are none other than those ominous gentiles encountered by the Jew in the gentile world is an interpretation not easy to avoid. It is imposed by that archetypal contrast in Chaplin films between the bloated, dough-colored Goliaths and the small, dark David-tramp. As to that black bowler in that ragged context, it is reminiscent of those turn-of-the-century photographs showing Jewish peddlers whose black bowlers, substituting for the more traditional black felt hats, are the first concession to "secularism." Seen in this light, the relationship between the Chaplin tramp and the millionaire in *City Lights* becomes the gist of the Jews' history in Europe: when he is drunk, and in need of someone, the millionaire embraces the tramp and takes him into his house; next morning, when he is sober and self-sufficient, he promptly kicks the tramp into the street. On the other hand, as James Agee says about the tramp in *City Lights*, "it has never occurred to him that he is inadequate." (3, p. 10) There is an echo here of that *élan* of Sholom Aleichem's Menachem Mendel, who comes to the city of Odessa in order to become a millionaire without a moment's doubt that he is "entitled."

A less symbolic and more direct relationship to Jewish ambiguity may be discernible in the slouching, bespectacled, cigar-puffing figure of Groucho Marx. He too is out to deflate pomposity and defeat villainy, yet he is also a recognizable Jewish con-man. His con game, however, is primarily one of identity: he is the transparently fraudulent possessor of names like Dr. Hackenbush, Professor Wagstaff, J. Cheever Loophole. He is obviously not what he claims to be, but he has few illusions about the acceptance of his claims. "Hooray for Captain Spaulding, the African explorer!" a crowd sings in *Animal Crackers*, welcoming him, and he sings back with mock outrage, "Did someone call me *shnorrer?*" He may pretend to be explorer, doctor, professor, but he slouches around quite openly as if weary of the impersonation. He is equally ironic about his own schemes; he starts out foxily on a clever course of action and ends up watching bemusedly how the "Italian" Chico and the deaf-mute Harpo cheat *him*. That resigned acceptance, that passive amusement in being defeated by others, coming as it does from one affecting all the mannerisms of the go-getting "shrewdie," sums up the comedy of Groucho and conceivably that of a certain ironic type of Jew still not fully at home in the secular Western world, ambitious, yet skeptical of the *value* of his own ambitions. The joke is here directed at both the presumption of the outsider in striving for exalted goals, as well as at those goals themselves, with their baggage of vanity, pomposity, futility.

To cite one more example of an "authentic" purveyor of Jewish comedy, i.e. comedy reflecting the Jewish condition and the resultant special perspective, one might jump ahead a few decades to Lenny Bruce. In his last phase Bruce had turned from standard, non-involved, Jewish Comedian to a speechifying comic Jeremiah, in trouble with the authorities. For whatever reason, there bubbled to the surface of Bruce's act what should according to the rules remain at the bottom of the entertainer's consciousness (provided there is something there). The frenzied resentments of the Yiddish-speaking immigrants' offspring, against the old world and the new, burst through the façade of that imitation Anglo-Saxon name and Bruce became, at least for a while, Louis Schneider again to the public. He proclaims it in a nightclub, somewhat incoherently, without prepared routine:

> Louis. That's my name in Jewish. Louis Schneider.
> "Why haven't ya got Louis Schneider up on the marquee?"
> "Well, cause it's not show business. It doesn't fit."
> "No. No. I don't wanna hear that. You Jewish?"
> "Yeah."
> "You ashamed of it?"
> "Yeah."
> "Why you ashamed you're Jewish?"
> "I'm not any more! But it used to be a problem. Until *Playboy* magazine came out."
> Yeah. That's right. You just can't be that urbane bachelor

and drive down the street driving a Jag or a Lotus yelling "nigger" and "kike." It don't really fit.

(19, p. 42)

Here is the imaginative kid from the immigrant neighborhood talking with a feverish "knowingness" in front of the candy store, confused about gentiles, hating his Jewishness and loving it too, as in the following monologue of re-definition:

> I neologize Jewish and *goyish*. Dig: I'm Jewish. Count Basie's Jewish. Ray Charles is Jewish. Eddie Cantor's *goyish*. Bnai Brith is *goyish;* Hadassah, Jewish. Marine Corps—heavy *goyim,* dangerous. Koolaid is *goyish*. All Drake's cakes are *goyish*. Pumpernickel is Jewish, and, as you know, white bread is very *goyish*. Instant potatoes—*goyish*. Black cherry soda's very Jewish, Macaroons are very Jewish—very Jewish cake. Fruit salad is Jewish. Lime jello is *goyish*. Lime soda is very *goyish*. Trailer parks are so *goyish* that Jews won't go near them.
>
> (19, p. 4)

The involvement here with Jewishness is genuine and the attempt to come to terms with it honest. But such involvement and honesty are quite out of place in the standard manner of the Jewish Comedian, a role Bruce in fact stopped playing as he moved toward authenticity in public.

Another type of divergence from that standard role of Jewish Comedian is represented by those Jews in comedy who strive for "universality." Bruce says quite justly that "Eddie Cantor is *goyish*," since Cantor's *persona* was, despite his publicized off-stage involvement in Jewish causes, that of an ethnically unspecific bumpkin of bug-eyed innocence. Similarly, Jack Benny has become a national symbol of genial stinginess that represents a human, rather than a more narrowly Jewish, proclivity. Perhaps in order to emphasize their own universality both comedians for years included comic Jews of ethnic flavor in their situation comedies: Cantor had his "Mad Russian" and Benny had Mr. Kitzel.

While comedians like Cantor and Benny are (or were) essentially "book" comedians—surrounding themselves regularly with casts that set up comic situations in which each star's respective stage personality can be displayed—the Jewish Comedian is typically a "stand-up" comedian, a man who appears on the "floor" and then stands and addresses the audience as "himself." He does not pretend to impersonate a character; he does not bring with him a cast and a play of which he is a part. Rather he implicitly asks the audience to become his passive cast, since he talks directly *to* the audience rather than to other actors. A situation is here created that seems to call for greater "honesty" on the part of the performer, since he cannot fall back on the make-believe of the play or playlet. Certainly the entire demeanor of the stand-up comedian as well as the *form* of his discourse is that of a man who is making a *personal* approach. When he begins to recite his gags, it is to "a listener" he has greeted, has introduced himself to, as it were, and has an apparent desire to communicate with. Moreover, the very fact that the communication generally is in a hearty, confidential tone—and most often concerns his own "life"—or at least his personal and private views on life—suggests that the comedian is talking to a listener he has somehow come to trust and, in fact, like. The stand-up comic's image is honest, hearty, loving.

Yet the fact is the stand-up comic is looking into the blackness of a cavernous nightclub, if he is not looking into the cold glass eye of a TV camera. All of that personal bonhomie is directed at nobody he can, in fact, see. He does not even have the minimal reality of a fellow actor to address and respond to. That warm, confidential, man-to-man manner vis-à-vis the audience thus actually involves a *greater* amount of make-believe than does play-acting, for it means playing opposite a "cast" (i.e. the audience) that is not only unknown to the comedian and essentially invisible, but that also may not, in its remoteness, collaborate, by laughing, in that scene of cozy communication the comedian attempts to set up, and then proceeds to pretend exists, whether or not it in fact does.

The implicitly claimed honesty of the stand-up comedian is thus inherently tainted. If a sense of make-believe adheres to the "reality" of a stage play, a sense of dishonesty adheres to the reality created by the comedian, precisely because it is claimed to be a genuine reality. The comedian's role, in this respect, has certain similarities to that of the salesman. The latter also comes as "himself," and he also attempts to be the "friend" of the potential customer. Yet he too, though pretending friendship, sees not a friend, perhaps not even a person, but simply a prospect; and he too, like the stand-up comedian, pretends that friendship indiscriminately, to everyone he approaches. In view of these similarities, it may not be fortuitous that salesmen tell a lot of jokes. The reverse is also true: the stand-up comedian comes on like a salesman; he comes *selling* his jokes.

One may surmise that the habit of comedians to refer to what they do as "work," as in "O.K., folks, now let me go to work," has to do with their partial self-image as salesmen. But more significantly, the "work" attitude points to an orientation that is the very opposite of that antic abandon characteristic of the classic buffoon, the congenital outsider to whom the framework of social reality is at best an insufferable cage. The buffoon does not *want* to belong, he does not curry favor, and what he above all does *not* do, or does not admit to doing, is "work"—which is after all what all those *inside* the cage do. The stand-up comedian, however, being really a salesman at heart, is concerned above all to show that he is a "regular guy" who believes in everything the audience believes in. The comedian is inside that cage and happy to be there and begging not to be ejected because of his levity. He proves his desire to belong by letting it be quite clearly understood that gag-telling is really only another way of selling, of working to make a buck. Honestly, folks!

What is most relevant here is that within the framework of the situation as defined by the *persona* of the stand-up comedian, nothing he talks about, whether it be his Jewishness, his family, his politics, is really more than a means to an end, which is laughter. The thing discussed is not important; the resultant sale, the laughter, is. So that the family, for example—a favorite subject because it can evoke sympathy in the audience as well as laughter—that family is never more than a phantasmagoria of comic cut-outs. When the *"goyish"* Eddie Cantor talked of his family, the country knew that he was talking about real people. When Alan King talks about his family, the audience can only picture indistinct grotesques; King's *real* family remains unknown, if indeed it exists. So also with the matter of Jewishness. Its avowal is meant to appear as a form of confiding, but since it comes from the heart of a salesman, it is after all only a confidence *trick*. When Don Rickles, a Jewish Comedian, scores a point off his "host"

Johnnie Carson and shouts "That's one for the Jewish kid," the mechanical nature of the remark is enough to make one doubt that Rickles is Jewish at all. When London Lee, a Jewish Comedian, relates how at his sister's wedding a mishap "blew up the rabbi and two ushers," the remark is so obviously machine-made to sell that one tends to believe that Lee's sister, if he should have one, surely got married, if she ever did, before a justice of the peace. The point is, the authenticity of the Jewish Comedian is so drastically threadbare that there is nothing really Jewish about his "Jewish humor."

Be that as it may, the role of Jewish Comedian is nevertheless the only role in which the Jew appears *as* Jew in the popular culture, pinning on himself a label of identity, tacitly claiming a valid relevance of that identity to the comic point of view. And there is indeed a precedent for the role in the Jewish past; for centuries before the emergence from ghetto and *shtetl,* there had been an institutionalized jester in Jewish community life. He was called *badkhen or marshallik.* "In the later middle ages the *marshallik* became an indispensable guest at any Jewish wedding. He was a merry jester to whom the utmost license was allowed, none being safe from his ready and often caustic wit. Not even the bride herself was spared, and many a time in the middle ages the *marshallik* obeyed the stern "forbear to exaggerate" of Shammai and, holding the mirror up to nature, told an ugly bride the truth. . . . But these liberties were rarer than the praises. 'Every bride is beautiful,' said Hillel, and most medieval *marshalliks* accepted this rose-colored axiom" (1, p. 198). Whatever the status of the *marshallik* as social critic, he stood of course totally within the community; the Jewish Comedian's Jewish identity, however, is problematic. He is no longer a *Jewish* institution; he is a creation of the popular culture. And so there is a precariousness in that Jewish identity, not however in the sense associated with a Lenny Bruce, or the humorists of earlier times like Heine, where there is a struggle to understand and come to terms. That precariousness has to do with the dubious salesman's "sincerity" that is the stock attitude of the Jewish Comedian. If confiding that he is Jewish is part of that sincerity, then the way Jewishness is used reflects the dishonesty of that sincerity.

For the sake of a better understanding of the social-psychological mechanisms at work in the creation of the Jewish Comedian, it might be useful here to attempt a brief sketch of an imaginary, abnormally long-lived individual's transformation, in terms of subjective experience, from *marshallik* to Jewish Comedian. One might thus see the marshallik, at home in the Jewish world, move from the *shtetl* to a large city, say, in Central Europe. There he at first continues to amuse crowds at Jewish weddings. Yet he is disturbed, since the urban environment releases larger ambitions. He begins to think of larger crowds and larger rewards. He thus expands his activity to include evenings of entertainment under the auspices of Jewish organizations. He is still dissatisfied, however, and as his command of the local language improves, he begins to move on to the variety or cabaret stages. He now begins to face larger audiences than ever, no longer exclusively Jewish, however, and of somewhat dubious sympathies. The laughter at Jewish jokes is still there, but the motivation does not seem entirely benevolent, as in the past. Still, it is the laughter that counts, that makes it possible to be a success, to make a good living. He thus makes no drastic efforts to change his style, even if that were possible. He does not stop being Jewish. Yet he finds that the stage Jew, though he provokes laughter, is not an object of love. The performer, however, needs love, he wants not to be laughed *at* but laughed *with*. And so the temptation arises for this comedian to propitiate the audience, to win it over to himself, personally, by subtly disassociating himself from the basically disliked Jew he embodies. The comedian therefore begins to make jokes concerning Jews in such a way as if to say "Look, I'm really laughing at them myself. I'm a little bit on *your* side." At this point, though he may also defy his audience by attacking what *it* stands for, the comedian has arrived at the point where he is no longer saying, as he did when still a *marshallik*, "How funny *certain* Jews are!" but where he is saying, in effect, "How funny the *Jews* are!" Herewith, the Jewish Comic Image is on the horizon.

At this juncture the comedian is still in Europe, possibly pre-World War II, and if he can be imagined transplanted now to contemporary American show business, he must probably be imagined as sensing a much less charged atmosphere in relation to his Jewishness, a veritable absence of that antagonism he sensed in the European audience. Yet, strangely enough, his laughs in connection with Jewishness come easier. He doesn't have to try as hard as he did in Europe to work up "clever" Jewish routines. Now he only has to say "Jewish"—so to speak— and a laugh follows. Paradoxically, he finds, he can now, should he want to, stop thinking along lines of Jewish humor specifically and just simply *refer*, without any more mental or emotional involvement, to Jewishness. He has, in short, come face to face with the ultimate Jewish Comic Image. And he thus becomes this chapter's ideal-typical Jewish Comedian.

CONCLUSION

ON THE BASIS OF THE POPULAR CULTURE SURVEY CONSTItuting the first part of the study, it can be confirmed that the media indeed not only convey a comic picture of the Jew, as expected, but that there exists a Jewish Comic Image, in the sense that the Jewish image is more comic than that of any other group, and that the Jewish humor does not demonstrably arise out of a distinct Jewish position in the larger society, or out of specifically Jewish idiosyncrasy. To be sure, there were instances of the "serious" Jew, especially in books, though even here the comic Jew dominates. Moreover, examples of a "valid" Jewish humor do still show up, though more in some media than in others. The comical dialect-speaking Jew, bearer most often of whimsical attitudes and ancient wisdom, is a character who still seems to appear rather frequently in plays, for example, possibly because the relatively limited and largely Jewish audience of the New York theatre may still cherish the memory of that particular type. On television, conversely, that type does not exist at all; its place is taken by the sleek, "Americanized" Jewish Comedian, purveyor of the Jewish Comic Image.

Of course both the old "ethnic" furniture dealer of Arthur Miller's *The Price*, for example, and a Jewish Comedian's glib reference to "my rabbi" cause laughter, since both jar the nervous system through incongruity. Yet the two reactions nevertheless differ fundamentally: the furniture dealer is perceived as being, in his way, "superior" to society, the comedian's rabbi as "inferior." The laughter provoked by the former's incongruity contains admiration for that very attribute, it being perceived as a form of intransigence, of rugged individualism; the laughter aroused by the comedian's rabbi derives from the vague notion that had the rabbi been smarter he might have become a comedian, or at least a "regular guy." It is this latter kind of laughter, one of derogation rather than admiration, that is typically invited to accompany the Jewish Comic Image.

In the historical section of this study, the attempt was made to show that what is known as Jewish Humor, and finally the Jewish Comic Image itself, must be associated with the historical circumstances pertaining to the Jew in modern Europe. Specifically, it is the frame of mind of an "uncomfortable" minority that results in the Jewish joke, and that discomfort can emerge both out of a strained sense of being in "exile," as was the case in Russia, as well as out of a strained sense of being "at home," as was the case in Germany. But the Russian exile involved at most a questioning only of Jewish "chosenness" in view of day-to-day indignities and deprivations; the German home involved the question of Jewish identity itself. Thus, Jewish Humor, growing in the gap between the ideal and the real, was a staple of Eastern Europe, but the Jewish Comic Image, bearing the notion that being Jewish is absurd, was typical only of Central Europe.

CONCLUSION

America was different. The Jew came to a place that was neither intent upon keeping him apart and oppressed, as Russia was, nor upon upholding the singularity of its culture and the holiness of its soil, as Germany was. In America a precedent existed for the possibility of being a 100-percent American who is nevertheless "hyphenated." There was no "official" position, certainly, contravening the notion that the Jew could be at home in America and yet be a Jew. There were of course other pressures contravening it, not least important the Jew's own uncertainty, brought from modern Europe, as to *how* to be a Jew. And a great part of that uncertainty was given verbal expression by the humor in which it had been "packed" and finally transported across the seas. Even some of this "valid" humor, however it reflected genuine inner perplexities, soon outlived its own relevancy, though it may persist to this day. Anti-rabbinical humor, for example, having evolved originally in an environment of occasionally stifling rabbinical authority, seems hardly appropriate to an American scene where rabbis often barely survive the whims of their congregations. But there was even less in the American climate that, in the light of the preceding historical analysis, would lead one to expect the emergence of the Jewish Comic Image, reflecting the absurdity of Jewish identity as such. There can be little doubt but that at least the core of the attitude behind that Image, originating among German Jews, must simply also have been brought along around the turn of the century; or perhaps it was brought even earlier, by the German Jews of the 19th century the way one might thoughtlessly bring galoshes to the desert. But if so, its strident manifestation in the media today would appear to be a very strange instance of "cultural lag," for one is faced not only with the continuation but the luxurious thriving of an attitudinal phenomenon that does not seem to be inherent in the social situation.

This question of the *flourishing* Jewish Comic Image will be examined somewhat later, but first it should be noted that as soon as one admits the possibility of a cultural lag, namely that this Jewish self-irony is a cultural trait of which neither source nor survival is directly attributable to the way America "treats" the Jew, then there is no longer necessarily a contradiction between the thesis of growing Jewish "normalization" and the existence of that self-irony. One begins to see two separate social impulses at work, proceeding from opposite directions. On one side, the American mechanisms of immigrant absorption provoke the transformation of all members of ethnic groups into Americans of specific religious denominations; on the other side the Jew proves incapable of fitting perfectly into this American pattern. He holds on, for one thing, to an ironic self-image that militates ultimately both against the "respectability" of Judaism and against the perfect Americanization of the Jew.

Seen in this way, as an "independent" cultural residue, Jewish self-irony is a phenomenon perhaps not unlike the persistent and rather self-destructive Irish tendency toward alcoholism. "Drink," writes Daniel P. Moynihan concerning the Irish in America, "has been their curse. It is the principal fact of Irishness that they have not been able to shake" (71). Drink, he maintains, is in fact the reason the Irish have not competed very successfully against the Jews in politics and the professions. "In ways it is worse now than in the past: a stevedore could drink and do his work; a lawyer, a doctor, a legislator cannot." But just as drinking is, as Moynihan suggests, a way of maintaining a sense of being Irish, self-irony may be a way of maintaining a sense of being Jewish. Certainly laughing at oneself, as was shown, had become in the 19th century a very intrinsic part of Jewish behavior, as much a cultural Jewish trait, in fact, as the Jewish religion itself, or the Yiddish language, or Zionism, or the proclivity for socialist ideologies.

What seems to have happened in America, however, is that of all these traits it was self-irony that had the best chance of survival. The Yiddish culture of New York during the early part of the century certainly had no such chance, and neither did socialism or Zionism (in the sense of a movement of mass emigration from America). These, as Herberg and others imply, run hopelessly counter to the American integrative processes. What America did officially support and "certify" as Jewish was the Jewish religion. Yet to the Jewish immigrants America, paradoxically, was a land where, though one remained a Jew, one was likely to drop religious observances. The very fact of going to America constituted a sort of defiance of religious traditions, which not infrequently had become bound up in the immigrants' vision with the oppressions and economic misery of the country left behind. Furthermore, religion seemed to stand in the way of realizing those hopes of material success engendered by America. And indeed, as was seen earlier (cf. Humor of the Cities), the Jewish immigrant subculture on the lower East Side was not first and foremost a religious one, and it threatened to become even less so with the coming of age of the second generation.

Nevertheless, what actually happened, of course, as the century progressed was that the essentially religious identity prescribed by the American milieu also became the only "natural" one for the Jew: no alternative self-definition, whether racial, national, or cultural, seemed quite so viable. And so the synagogues have increased and the membership figures have swelled. Yet religion is now much more a matter of social organization than of inner conviction. Herberg shows that of all religious groups in America, Jews *believe* the least. And the deadly earnest of old is no longer present even in the synagogue. In those mountain retreats, on the other hand, where vacationing American Jews may be said to have been most "genuinely" themselves, it is not the rabbi but the comedian who officiates, and the daily liturgy is not the Hebrew prayer but the comic monologue.

Although religion, then, is the official tag of the Jew in American society, his consciousness cannot be characterized as religious. It might more justly be characterized as ironic-about-itself. Now, if this self-irony is in fact a Jewish tradition, it has also turned out to be the tradition most readily available to the American Jew for reinforcing an inner sense of group identity. According to this analysis, self-irony should now survive among Jews even in the most "benign" of environments, outside Israel. (*There* running the country itself is of course a means of sustaining a sense of group identity.) Yet American society does after all seem to become implicated in the maintenance of the Jewish ironic consciousness, if only indirectly so: the very fact that there is not a precise correspondence between the "official" American definition of the Jew and his inner perception of himself must become a source of sustenance for that irony. And in this way American society may be said to contribute after all to the creation of the Jewish Comic Image. But it is a rather indirect role American society plays here, since

CONCLUSION

there is a basic consistency between America's proclamation of the Jew's equal religious status and its presumed readiness to accept that status. Unlike pre-Hitler Germany, for example, which never accepted the "Germans of Mosaic faith" as Germans, America accepts its American Jews as Americans. The "problem" is thus primarily that of the Jew himself: his self-irony is largely self-perpetuated, though of course its hold may be unbreakable.

In returning now to the attempt at understanding the *flourishing* Jewish Comic Image, it is necessary to start with that great Jewish reservoir of self-irony. Here is a distinctive Jewish cultural possession one of whose concrete consequences is the existence in the world, and more relevantly America, of a disproportionately large number of Jewish comedians. But these not only embody that self-ironic impulse, they turn it into a profession that generates impulses of its own. As was shown earlier (cf. Humor of the Cities) the profession of the "parochial" Jewish comedian dictated appearances in Kansas City as well as the "mountains" and consequently dictated also the development of a humor of Jewishness *as such*. Thus the earlier flicker, one might say, of "arbitrary" irony concerning Jewish identity itself, part of the heritage of European Jewish self-irony, was gradually fanned into a flame in America through the vagaries of show business and, most decisively, through the "accident" of television.

According to this analysis, the Jewish Comic Image itself may thus actually no longer be *directly* dependent upon the survival of that traditional Jewish self-ironic impulse. The Image possibly has become a self-perpetuating "show biz" device. It certainly is no longer associated just with the Jewish Comedian but has become a resource of humor in all areas of entertainment.

What is of course impressed upon the public consciousness in the course of this institutionalization of what used to be an aspect of Jewish self-irony is the image of the Jew as somehow laughable as well as laughing. Now, in a social schema represented by Will Herberg's "triple melting pot," wherein the Jew is no more and no less than the embodiment of one of the three major religions, that comic image must of course prove "dysfunctional." It contradicts the notion that the Jew has an identity to be taken as "seriously" as that of other Americans. It necessarily reinforces, if it does not create, gentile latent anti-Semitism as well as Jewish self-irony, for quite inevitably that image, purveyed over the media, becomes a major source of "information" about the Jew, both for the Jew himself and for the non-Jew.

Moreover, what is considered comic may shade easily into what is considered pernicious. An instance of how the Jewish Comic Image may function in the formation of attitudes is provided by a recent (November 1969) radio commercial for the Youth Corps. A mother is heard talking to someone on the other end of the phone. She is complaining that her son, after all she has done for him, is "throwing his life away" by joining the Youth Corps. The mother here is of course the villainess, meant to offset all the positive values the Youth Corps is proclaimed to stand for. Significantly, in this commercial she is portrayed as a *Jewish* mother.

Insofar as this study has traced the persistence of a collective self-image, there are perhaps wider implications. For instance, one might apply some of these insights to the American Negro. While this is not the place to pursue the matter with any thoroughness, it might be suggested that in the case of the Negro too there is evidence of a persistent self-image—in this case the negative, self-deprecatory one acquired during slavery—which seems to survive *despite* counter-indicatory changes in social context. To wit, the posture of Black Power, with its segregatory implications (in the face of an objectively accelerated movement in American society since the middle fifties toward greater integration) might be seen in part as a manifestation of a tenacious negative self-image. For if the Negro, due in part to that self-image, cannot help but feel *uncomfortable* with the white, then he must feel so especially if the latter should attempt to "come closer".

Of course one must keep in mind that this is at most only part of the picture, that a lingering black self-image would necessarily have to be understood as the counterpart of a lingering white image of the blacks. Yet it might be useful to look at such a self-image by itself in order to comprehend its separate destructive potential, the way this was attempted here in the case of the Jewish experience. Saying "Black is beautiful" is of course an attempt to neutralize a negative self-image, but it would probably take a very deliberate and courageous grappling with such an image before the black could truly accept his own "beauty" or the Jew could do without any irony in order to be himself.

APPENDIX

New York Plays of Six Seasons 1964–65 to 1969–70

THE FOLLOWING LIST CONSISTS OF PLAYS WITH JEWISH characters. After each title follows a short description of the play and, frequently, a short relevant quote from reviewers' comments. Where the Jewishness of a character was suggested *only* by a name,=i.e. *Dear Janet Rosenberg, Dear Mr. Kooning* (1969–70), the play was not included. Revivals (i.e. *Room Service, Awake and Sing,*) also were not listed and neither were plays whose Jewish characters turned out to be of minuscule importance. For example, in the musical *Company* (1969–70) a young bride, herself a minor character, reveals quite incidentally that the man she is about to marry —another character in the play—is a Jew and that *she* is Catholic. She makes the comic remark that when she started going with this man she felt, "I had my own *Jew!*" But neither before nor after this minuscule interlude is the religious identity of either character broached, nor does it play any further role whatsoever in the play. *Company* is therefore not listed, though that small interlude happens to utilize in a small way that comic potential of Jewishness other plays utilize more thoroughly. Again, revues, such as *The Dirtiest Show in Town* (1969–70,) about which a critic said that "the jokes, almost exclusively homosexual and/or Jewish, are a matter less of words than of passwords." (*New Yorker*, July 4, 1970,) were not included, since there are, strictly speaking, no Jewish *characters*, and the nature of the individual jokes is not in every case ascertainable.

The major source for this list is the annual *Best Plays of*—compiled by Otis L. Guernsey, Jr. This source is supplemented by reviews in newspapers and periodicals.

1964–1965

Fiddler on the Roof. Musical built around Sholom Aleichem's character Tevye, 19th-century Russian Jewish milkman.

The Sign in Sidney Brustein's Window. About the struggles of a young Jewish editor of a Village newspaper; among his inspirations are the ancient Maccabees.

I Had A Ball. Musical comedy about Coney Island characters. Buddy Hackett, Jewish comedian, as Max, the Crystal Ball.

Odd Couple. Neil Simon, Broadway's top comedy playwright, "writing Jewish" (cf. Films).

The Day the Whores Came Out to Play Tennis. "Black" comedy about the destruction of a country club. The whores, who are never seen, are "the destroyers of the paradise that the Cherry Valley Country Club has been. ". . . Is there any special reason why the president and his committee—each with some variant of a Yiddish accent—should be the object of this visitation? . . . The members of the committee are obnoxious." (*New York Times*, March 16, 1965) "I haven't the faintest idea why the country club is Jewish, except that maybe Mr. Kopit [author] found it easier to make jokes in this atmosphere" (*Newsday,* March 16, 1965).

Square in the Eye. "Black" comedy about a young artist couple. The wife's parents "are cartoons of middle class New York Jews" (*Women's Wear Daily,* May 20, 1965). They "behave like a vaudeville team that specializes in Jewish dialect routines . . ." (*New York Times,* May 20, 1965). "The sort of obnoxious caricatures that were depicted by the Nazis" (*Newsday,* May 20, 1965). The play includes an actor "throwing the audience into successive stages of shock as a doctor, an undertaker, and the rabbi reading the funeral service [of the young wife]. That whole area of the play is the most eye-opening theatrical 'grotesque' of the season." (*New York World Telegram,* May 20, 1965).

Flora, the Red Menace. Musical about radicals of the thirties. Includes comic relief by an old Jewish clock repairman, a "stock old-world type."

1965–1966

Friends and Enemies. A double bill of one-acters, starring Jewish dialect comedian Eli Mintz. "The chief purpose served by the play is to put on view the considerable comic talents of Eli Mintz. . . . [In one play] he is called upon to depict that ancient and familiar comic character, the Jewish waiter" (*Herald Tribune,* September 27, 1965).

The Impossible Years. A comedy about a child psychologist having difficulties with his own offspring, starring Alan King. Perhaps the Jewishness here is most explicit in the casting.

The Exhaustion of Our Son's Love. "Black" comedy

about a Jewish family waiting for a son to return from a European hitch with the Army, learning at the end that the son has defected to the East. "A Goldbergs of the absurd" (*Women's Wear Daily*, October 19, 1965), in which "we are treated to a patter of Jewish jokes" (*New York Times*, October 19, 1965).

The Zulu and the Zayda. Comedy about a frisky Jewish grandpa in South Africa, starring Menasha Skulnik, Jewish dialect comedian, in which a Zulu becomes the old man's companion, learning Yiddish in the process. There is "condescension to Jewish customs and the cheap dependence . . . on Borscht Belt Yiddishisms . . . an encouragement of stereotype humor" (*Women's Wear Daily*, November 11, 1965).

The Pocket Watch. A "modest, tender Jewish domestic comedy." (*New York Post*, January 6, 1966). "Aaronson [author] manages to accurately reproduce the conversational patterns of a Jewish household, although these are clichés rather than dialogue and the characters are types rather than people—the pushy, the materialistic, the old world, and so on" (*Women's Wear Daily*, January 6, 1966).

Jonah. The biblical story, retold by Goodman in terms of "Jewish domestic folklore comedy" (*New York Post*, February 16, 1966). "Goodman has made Jonah a Yiddish-accent old man who not only tells bad jokes but dreams them" (*New York World Telegram*, February 16, 1966). Jonah becomes "a stock Hebrew comic. A part that cries out for Menasha Skulnik" (*Newsday*, February 16, 1966).

Nathan Weinstein, Mystic, Conn. A "sophisticated farce" concerning the Jewish tendency to assimilate, starring Jewish stage comedian Sam Levene in the title role.

Weinstein's son changes his name to Wang; Weinstein objects, his daughter is perplexed as to whose side to take.

Monopoly. Four Bronx pastiches, involving "sadness and comedy," such as that of "Princess Rebecca Birnbaum," whose innate good taste in dress is shattered by family and friends.

1966–1967

Don't Drink the Water. Comedy about a Jewish caterer from Newark and family, visiting Moscow, being mistaken for spies.

Cabaret. Musical which includes a Berlin landlady with a Jewish suitor. The time is shortly before the Nazi takeover. The suitor is played by Jack Gilford, Jewish comic actor, though the treatment of the story is not basically comic.

Chu Chem. (Closed before opening in New York.) Musical with Menasha Skulnik, about a Jewish family in China. The Chinese-sounding title is actually a Yiddish word, meaning approximately "wise guy."

Harold and Sondra. A double bill, dealing satirically, in "black" comedy fashion, with Jewish family manners and mores. In one the family casually continues squabbling while it is physically smothering young Harold, the son, to death.

1967–1968

Scuba Duba. Comedy about a Jewish American on the Riviera, who suspects that his wife has run off with a black skin diver. In his frenzy, the hero puts in a "transatlantic call to his Jewish mother, and a life-size cartoon cut-out of her slides onto the stage" (*Saturday*

Review, October 28, 1967). The hero is a kind of "Everyman as Jewish coward" (*Ibid.*).

Something Different. Comedy about a "blocked" Jewish writer who tries to re-create the circumstances under which he once wrote a successful play. After installing a run-down, old-fashioned kitchen in his elaborate quarters, he finds that "what is missing is his mother, grumbling, complaining, and singing her comforting Yiddish songs. . . . He goes to an employment agency, gets three women applicants, including a Yiddish-speaking Negro" (*New York Times*, September 29, 1967).

Walking to Waldheim. A "comedy almost to the end" about five bickering relatives accompanying H. Goldblatt to his wife's funeral.

How to Be a Jewish Mother. A string of comic sketches concerning the J.M., with Jewish stage comedienne Molly Picon. A Negro actor impersonated alternately the son and the husband. There was some "humorously defensive anti-Semitism" (*New York Times*, December 29, 1967).

Golden Rainbow. Musical about a Jewish entrepreneur struggling to run a resort hotel, while taking care of a little boy. "Sammy Glick on the loose in Las Vegas" (*New York Times*, February 5, 1968), involving "a collection of wise cracks and patter" (*Women's Wear Daily*, February 5, 1968).

The Price. About two brothers who meet in an attic to sell some jointly-owned furniture to an old Jewish dealer, a comedy character.

The Other Man. About Jewish survivors of Nazi death camps who find a war criminal being held prisoner in Buenos Aires.

Carry Me Back to Morningside Heights. Comedy about

a Jewish youth's insistence on becoming a slave to a Negro law student, as a kind of personal penance for historical wrongs. "Carp," the youth says at one point, "is the soul food of my people." He points out that he's a Jew, "but not Jewish."

Saturday Night. Comedy, with pathos, about an unhappy Bronx librarian who creates a dream world of imaginary "culture." While her widower father goes to Paradise (Loew's) on Saturday nights, she invites over another lonely girl for "literary conversation."

The Education of Hyman Kaplan. Musical about a comical but charming Jewish immigrant who goes to night school to study English and falls in love with a fellow student.

I'm Solomon. Musical about King Solomon and a cobbler who is the king's double, starring Dick Shawn.

The Latent Heterosexual. Comedy about a homosexual poet who is advised by his Jewish tax consultant to marry, for tax advantages. Subsequently the consultant advises divorce for the same reason. Finally: "Death would be a great tax advantage."

1968–1969

Play it Again, Sam. Comedy about a Jewish intellectual (played by Woody Allen) who invokes the ghost of Humphrey Bogart in order to overcome timidity in sexual pursuits.

Goodbye People. A "serious comedy" about an old Coney Island man, a "Jewish poppa full of life and spirit refusing to die" (*New York Times,* December 4, 1968), played by Milton Berle. "There are as many laughs as sea shells" (*Wall Street Journal,* December 5, 1968).

Jimmy Shine. The story of a young shlemiel, fumbling

in his painting and not getting the girl. The "biggest laughs are generated by the Yiddish comedian Eli Mintz as the proprietor of a fish store where Jimmy works briefly" (*Wall Street Journal,* December 9, 1968).

1969–1970

Show Me Where the Good Times Are. Musical comedy version of Molière's *Le Malade Imaginaire,* its setting transferred to the Jewish Lower East Side. The Jewishness is "merely slapped on, adventitiously and meretriciously." (*New York Magazine,* March 23, 1970).

The Penny Wars. About a boy's experiences in the thirties, including a stepfather who is a Jewish refugee dentist unable to adjust to the new American environment.

Butterflies Are Free. "A young man blind from birth escapes his horrible, dominating Jewish mother in the Bronx and sets himself up as a beginning songwriter in the Village." The mother's conversation consists of "wisecrack after wisecrack" (*The New Yorker,* November 1, 1969).

A Teaspoon Every Four Hours. Comedy with Jackie Mason, about a Jewish father who discovers his son is dating a black girl. "If a white, gentile, Protestant ever got off as many slanted racial and religious gags he might well be charged with offensive taste, if not bigotry" (*Variety,* June 18, 1969).

The Chinese and Dr. Fish. Two comic one-acters. One takes place in a Chinese laundry, where a Chinese couple turns out to have a "white" son who claims he is Jewish. The parents are shocked when he brings home a Jewish girl since they had hoped he would settle down with "a nice Chinese girl from Hong Kong" (*New York Times,*

March 11, 1970). The second comedy concerns one Charlotte Mendelsohn who comes to consult Dr. Fish (Ph.D. in history) concerning sexual fulfillment.

Inquest. The trial and execution of the Rosenbergs.

Engagement Baby. Comedy about a Jewish advertising executive who discovers to his dismay that he has an illegitimate black teen-age son. The play is "filled from start to finish with anti-Semitic wisecracks of a cheapness and viciousness that, if the author's name had been anything less than Shapiro, might well have caused him to suffer the ancient Wasp punishment of tar and feathers. Such jokes as were not aimed at mocking Jews were intended to encourage blacks" (*New Yorker,* May 30, 1970).

Paris is Out. "A traditional Jewish domestic comedy," with "incessant bickering" between "smothering mama, whining poppa, and anguished offspring" (*New Yorker,* February 7, 1970).

Norman, Is That You? Comedy about a Jewish drycleaner from Dayton who comes to New York to find his son has turned homosexual. The play is "written as a vehicle for Lou Jacobi, which turns it into a Jewish comedy, and creates an inherently funny situation—a Jewish father coping with a homosexual son, a tragedy far greater than marrying a Gentile (*Women's Wear Daily,* February 20, 1970). "The audience is evidently supposed to find 'fat,' 'middle-aged,' 'Jewish,' 'businessman,' 'Dayton,' 'Montreal,' and especially 'Julius' excrutiatingly funny" (*New Yorker,* February 28, 1970).

Last of the Red Hot Lovers. Neil Simon's comedy about Barney Cashman, a "fat and 47-year old schnook" (*Morning Telegraph,* December 30, 1969), owner of the Queen of the Sea Restaurant, who has been married for 23 years and attempts a last (and only) fling. "Ethnically, Simon's humor is Jewish, though not in the sense of dialect or in jokes. He is a master of the self-protective, self-deprecating, put-down. One makes a clown of oneself before anyone else does" (*Time,* January 12, 1970).

Minnie's Boys. Musical about the Marx Brothers and their mother-manager.

The following list consists of plays presenting non-Jewish ethnic characters.

1964–1965

Matty, the Moron, and the Madonna. About a "tenement child searching for outward signs of the peace instilled within him by his Roman Catholic religion" (*Christian Science Monitor,* April 6, 1965).

I Was Dancing. About an old Irish ex-vaudeville dancer. The old man, a sentimental figure, reminisces about his youth, philosophizes about old age. The comic highlight is supplied by the monologue concerning the death of a mutual acquaintance, delivered by a Jewish friend. However, "the character, thrown in purely for Jewish color, just doesn't say Jewish things, despite Eli Mintz's thick accent" (*Women's Wear Daily,* November 9, 1964).

1965–1966

Hogan's Goat. About a Brooklyn Irish politician of the early 1890s, "young, determined, driving, haranguing, remorselessly ambitious" (*Morning Telegraph,* November 13, 1965), "part of him is aflame with resentments . . . part of him reaches out for love" (*New York Times,* November 12, 1965). The dialogue abounds in "high-flown figures of speech" (*Ibid.*), each of the Irish characters being credited with poetic eloquence.

Minor Miracle. A comedy about a lovable old priest,

who has "a secret hunger for religious ecstasy" (*Village Voice*, October 14, 1965). The familiar comedy ingredients "include a Jewish druggist friend who keeps bringing in bagels and bourbon" (*Wall Street Journal*, October 11, 1965). However, this "chum is Jewish only in that he deletes the term 'of,' as in 'a bottle bourbon'" (*Women's Wear Daily*, October 8, 1965).

1966–1967

Not a Way of Life. The play deals with "the controversy between new, liberal elements in the church and the traditionalists over birth control." . . . There is "debate between husband and wife, wife and priest, and even priest and priest" (*Wall Street Journal*, March 24, 1967). There is also a funny Irish mother, "not [a figure] that we've seen recently" (*New York Times*, March 24, 1967), who advises her daughter that the best cure for a cold is Lourdes water.

That Summer—That Fall. The Tragedy of Phaedra transposed to a modern Italian family in New York.

1967–1968

Mike Downstairs. "Mulberry Street [as a] sunny corner of Sicily set in the dirty heart of New York. . . . Colorful characters: the man who always sleeps, the widow forever invoking God, the honest butcher, the tart of gold, . . . the comic priest, the fat man in love with the thin girl, Mike himself, fount of all human wisdom and a believer in Spinoza" (*New York Times*, April 19, 1968). Mike, played by dramatic actor Dane Clark, tries to convince his neighbors to ignore a Civil Defense drill and fails.

1969–1970

A Whistle in the Dark. Drama about "a pride of Irish gutter lions" (*Time,* October 17, 1969). A decent son tries to withstand his alcoholic father and corrupt brothers who move in on him and his wife.

Borstal Boy. Play about Brendan Behan's experiences in an English reformatory.

Cry for Us All. Musical version of the play *Hogan's Goat* (1965–66), whose "tragic theme" (*New York Times,* April 9, 1970) is Irish politics in the Brooklyn of the 1890s.

Child's Play. A horror story set in a Catholic school whose students have mysteriously turned evil.

Steam Bath. Comedy set in a steam bath, which is really heaven's vestibule, and whose Puerto Rican attendant is really God. However, God "is rather Jewish for a Puerto Rican: 'I can't get my fresh lox, I don't know why that is!' . . . There's a lot in the play that is bitter-funny Jewish" (*New York Post,* July 1, 1970).

BIBLIOGRAPHY

1. Abrahams, Israel, *Jewish Life in the Middle Ages*, New York, Meridian Books, 1958.
2. Adler, J. G., *Die Juden in Deutschland*, Munich, Kösel-Verlag, 1960.
3. Agee, James, *Agee on Film*, New York, McDowell Obolensky, 1958.
4. Aleichem, Sholom, *The Old Country*, New York, Crown Publishers, 1946.
5. ———, *Menachem Mendel*, New York, Morgen-Freiheit, 1937.
6. Allen, Steve, *The Funny Men*, New York, Simon and Schuster, 1956.
7. Ausubel, Nathan, *Treasury of Jewish Folklore*, New York, Crown, n.d.
8. Bach, Hans, *Jüdische Memoiren aus drei Jahrhunderten*, Berlin, Schocken Verlag, 1936.
9. Bellow, Saul, *Herzog, New York*, Viking, 1964.
10. Berelson, Bernard, *Content Analysis in Communications Research*, Glencoe, Ill., Free Press, 1952.
11. Berend, A. L., *Der Judische Spassvogel*, Munich, 1877.
12. Bloch, Chajim, *Ostjudischer Humor*, Berlin, B. Harz, 1920.

13. ——, *Hersh Ostropoler*, Vienna, B. Harz, 1921.
14. Brod, Max, *Heine: The Artist in Revolt*, New York, Collier, 1962.
15. Buber, Martin, *Die Chassidischen Geschichten*, Berlin, Schocken, 1927.
16. Burma, J. H., "Humor as a Technique in Racial Conflict," *American Soc. Review*, December 1946.
17. Chotzner, J., *Hebrew Humor*, London, 1905.
18. Cohen, Elliot E., "Letters to the Movie Makers," *Commentary*, August 1947.
19. Cohen, John, *The Essential Lennie Bruce*, New York, Ballantine, 1967.
20. Dawidowicz, Lucy S., "Explaining American Jews," *Commentary*, December 1968.
21. Drujanow, A., *Sefer Habdicha Vehachidud*, Tel Aviv, 1935.
22. Dubnow, S. M., *History of the Jews in Russia and Poland*, Philadelphia, Jewish Publication Society, 1920.
23. Eliot, George, *Impressions of Theophrastus Such*, New York, Thomas Nelson & Sons, 1925.
24. Eyles, Allen, *The Marx Brothers*, New York, A. S. Barnes, 1966.
25. Friedman, Bruce Jay, *Stern*, New York, New American Library, 1962.
26. ——, *Scuba Duba*, New York, Pocket Books, 1968.
27. ——, *A Mother's Kisses*, New York, Pocket Books, 1968.
28. Fuchs, E., *Die Juden in der Karikatur*, Munich, A. Langen, 1921.
29. Gilbert, Douglas, *American Vaudeville*, New York, McGraw-Hill, 1940.
30. Glazer, Nathan, *American Judaism*, Chicago, University of Chicago, 1957.

31. Glückel of Hameln, *The Life of Glückel of Hameln*, London, East and West Library, 1962.
32. Goldman, William, *The Season*, New York, Harcourt, Brace & World, 1969.
33. Goldstein, S., and C. Goldscheider, *Jewish Americans*, Englewood Cliffs, N.J., Prentice-Hall, 1968.
34. Graetz, H., *History of the Jews*, Philadelphia, Jewish Publication Society, 1891.
35. Green, Abel and Joe Laurie Jr., *Show Biz*, New York, Henry Holt & Co., 1951.
36. Greenberg, Dan, *How to be a Jewish Mother*, New York, Pocket Books, 1965.
37. Greenburg, Clement, review of *Royte Pomerantzen*, *Commentary*, December 1947.
38. Gronemann, S., *Schalet*, Berlin, Jüdischer Verlag, 1927.
39. Gross, Heinrich, *Die Satire in der Judischen Literatur*, 1908.
40. Grotjahn, Martin, *Beyond Laughter*, New York, McGraw-Hill, 1957.
41. Guernsey, Otis L. Jr., *Best Plays of 1964 (1965, 1966, 1967, 1968)*, New York, Dodd, Mead & Co., 1964–68.
42. Guiles, Fred L., *Norma Jean*, New York, McGraw-Hill, 1969.
43. Hackett, Alice P., *70 Years of Best Sellers, 1895–1965*, New York, R. R. Bowker, 1967.
44. Halkin, Simon, *Modern Hebrew Literature*, New York, Schocken, 1950.
45. Hapgood, Hutchins, *Spirit of the Ghetto*, New York, Funk and Wagnalls, 1965.
46. Heine, Heinrich, *Gesammelte Werke*, vol. 3, Berlin, Grote'sche Verlagsbuchhandlung, 1887.
47. Herberg, Will, *Protestant, Catholic, Jew*, New York, Anchor Books, 1960.

48. "Humor" article in *International Encyclopedia of Social Sciences*, New York, McMillan Co., & Free Press, 1968.
49. Isaacs, A. S., *Rabbinical Humor*, New York, 1893.
50. *Jewish Book Annual*, vol. 25, New York, Jewish Book Council of America, 1967.
51. Kael, Pauline, *I Lost it at the Movies*, New York, Atlantic Monthly Press, 1965.
52. ———, *Kiss Kiss Bang Bang*, New York, Bantam Books, 1968.
53. Kahn, L., "The Jewish Novel," *Catholic World*, January 1967.
54. Kazin, Alfred, "The Jew as Modern Writer," *Commentary*, April 1966.
55. Klapp, Orin E., *Heroes, Villains, and Fools*, Englewood Cliffs, N.J., Prentice-Hall, 1962.
56. Kohn, Jacob P., *Rabbinischer Humor aus alter und neuer Zeit*, Berlin, 1915.
57. Kopit, Arthur, *The Day the Whores Came Out to Play Tennis*, New York, Hill and Wang, 1964.
58. Kristol, Irving, "Is Jewish Humor Dead?", *Commentary*, November 1951.
59. Landmann, Salcia, *Jiddisch*, Munich, Deutscher Taschenbuch Verlag, 1964.
60. ———, *Der Judische Witz*, Olten, Walter-Verlag, 1960.
61. Levenson, Sam, "The Dialect Comedian Should Vanish," *Commentary*, August 1952.
62. Lindzey, G., ed., "Humor," in *Handbook of Social Psychology*, Cambridge, Addison-Wesley, 1954.
63. Liptzin, Sol, *The Flowering of Yiddish Literature*, New York, Thomas Yoseloff, 1963.
64. ———, *Germany's Stepchildren*, New York, Meridian Books, 1961.

65. Loewe, Heinrich, *Agada*, Reichenberg, 1931.
66. McLean, Albert F., *American Vaudeville as Ritual*, Lexington, University of Kentucky Press, 1965.
67. Mersand, Joseph, *The American Drama Presents the Jew*, New York, The Modern Chapbook, 1939.
68. Miller, Arthur, *The Price*, New York, Bantam Books, 1968.
69. Morgan, Paul, Robitschek, Kurt, *Die Einsame Träne*, Berlin, 1924.
70. Moszkowski, Alexander, *Der Judische Witz und seine Philosophie*, Berlin, 1923.
71. Moynihan, Daniel P., "The Irish of New York," *Commentary*, August 1963.
72. Peters, M. C., *Wit and Wisdom of the Talmud*, New York, 1900.
73. Popkin, Henry, "The Vanishing Jew of our Popular Culture," *Commentary*, July, 1952.
74. *Publishers' Weekly*.
75. Reitzer, A., *Gut Yontev*, Pressburg, 1899.
76. Rezzori, Gregor von, "Memoirs of an Anti-Semite," *The New Yorker*, April 26, 1969.
77. Ringer, Benjamin B., *The Edge of Friendliness: A Study of Jewish-Gentile Relations*, New York, Basic Books, 1967.
78. Roback, A. A., *Curiosities of Yiddish Literature*, Cambridge, Mass., Sci-Art Publishers, 1933.
79. ———, *Story of Yiddish Literature*, New York, Yiddish Scientific Institute, 1940.
80. Rogow, Arnold A., *The Jew in a Gentile World*, New York, MacMillan Company, 1961.
81. Rosenberg, B., and Shapiro, G., "Marginality and Jewish Humor," *Midstream*, Spring, 1958.
82. Ross, George, "Death of a Salesman in the Original," *Commentary*, February 1951.

83. Roth, Philip, *Portnoy's Complaint*, New York, Random House, 1969.
84. Sanders, Ronald, *The Downtown Jews*, New York, Harper and Row, 1969.
85. Saphir, M. G., *Humoristisches Allerlei*, Vienna, 1897.
86. Schary, Dore, "Letter from a Movie-Maker," *Commentary*, October 1947.
87. Schiessler, S. W., *Frische Judenkirschen*, Meissen, 1827.
88. *Schlemiel*, Illustriertes jüdisches Witzblatt, Berlin, 1906.
89. Scholem, Gerschom G., *Major Trends in Jewish Mysticism*, New York, Schocken, 1954.
90. Selznick, Gertrude J., and Stephen Steinberg, *The Tenacity of Prejudice*, New York, Harper and Row, 1969.
91. Shubow, J. S., "Isaac Erter," *Reflex*, February 1929.
92. Simmons, Charles, *Powdered Eggs*, New York, E. P. Dutton & Co., 1964.
93. Simon, Sol, *The Wise Men of Chelm*, New York, Behrman House, 1955.
94. Sklare, Marshall, and Joseph Greenblum, *Jewish Identity on the Suburban Frontier*, New York, Basic Books, 1967.
95. Solotaroff, Theodore, review of *Herzog*, *Commentary*, December 1964.
96. Stember, H. C., *Jews in the Mind of America*, New York, Basic Books, 1966.
97. Tarr, Herbert, *Heaven Help Us*, New York, Bantam Books, 1967.
98. Tornabene, Lyn, *What's a Jewish Girl?*, New York, 1966.
99. Updike, John, *Bech: A Book*, New York, Alfred A. Knopf, 1970.

100. Wilde, Larry, *The Great Comedians Talk About Comedy*, New York, Citadel Press, 1968.
101. Weinberg, Herman G., *The Lubitsch Touch*, New York, E. P. Dutton & Co., 1968.
102. Wirth, Louis, *The Ghetto*, Chicago, Phoenix Books, 1956.
103. Yaffe, James, *The American Jews*, New York, Paperback Library, 1969.
104. Zborowski, Mark and Elizabeth Herzog, *Life is with People: The Culture of the Shtetl*, New York, Schocken, 1952.

INDEX

Abie's Irish Rose, 49
Ability *not* to contend against fate or society, 132
Absconded wife theme, 60, 61
Academy Awards ball, 83
Acculturation, 105
Adams, Joey, 186
Aleichem, Sholom, 18, 153–59, 188, 207; *the* classic writer of the Jews in modern times and a comic writer, 18; self-affirming, a literature of consolation, 154; joyful humor of, and comedy with the vitality of the totally powerless, 155; character of Menachem Mendel, 156; ex-exchange of his world for Heine's, 159; settling in New York, 159
Allen, Woody (public *persona* as Jewish comedian), 61, 186, 212
Allen, Steve ("most comedians are Jewish"), 186
All My Sons, 52
American identity of the Jew, 18
Americanization: ethnically neutral humor of Wynn, Cantor, Benny, Kaye, 169; generational conflict triggered, 161; satirical humor becomes domesticated, 169
American Jew: hero in films only if comic hero, 37; late forties first acknowledgment of existence of, 33
American Jewish Committee poll, 14
Amsterdam, Morey, 186
The Angel Levine, 37, 39, 46, 120
Angoff, Charles, 102
Animal Crackers, 188
Anti-Jewish attitudes (possible persisting latency), 15; anti-Semitic humor, 23; reflection of reality of inter-group tensions, 23–24; submerged into covert channels, such as laughter, 19
Anti-rabbinical humor, 45–46, 186, 199
Anti-Semites, 123; jokes of, 123; humor of, 172–81; caricatures to support hatred, 172–73; money-lending motif, 174; "realistic" approach, 174; the *shlemiel,* 175; the traditional ghetto Jew, 175. *See also* Jewish nose

225

Anti-Semitic jokes (from an Austrian collection), 177–79. *See also* Anti-Jewish attitudes
Anti-Semitism, 14, 15, 19, 23, 33, 38
Anti-Semitism of Jews: forced, 165; imagined, 165
The Apartment, 36
"Arbitrary" Jewish humor: cliché of the "nincompoop"
Awake and Sing, 67

Baby Hip, 115
A Bad Man, 115
Baker, Phil, 186
Ballard, Kaye, 80
Barefoot in the Park, 61
Baron, Sandy, 186
Bech: A Book, 116–18
Beggar in Jerusalem, 100
Behan, Brendan, 217
Bellow, Saul, 104
Benny, Jack ("universal" point of view), 78, 79, 169, 185, 186, 190–91
Berelson, 25
Berle, Milton, 186, 212
Berman, Shelley, 76, 186
Berry, Dave, 91, 98
Bible, humor in, 126–28
Bishop, Joey, 73, 76, 78, 81, 98, 186
Black comedian (satirizes the white man), 87
The Black Moritz, 169
Blintzkrieg, 102
Blue, Ben, 186
Body and Soul, 33
Boerne, Ludwig, 144
Bogart, Humphrey, 212
Books, 100
Borstal Boy, 217

Boyle, Peter, 97, 99
Braverman, Martin, 96, 99
Bruce, Lenny, 186, 189–90, 195
Burns, George, 78, 89, 186
Burrows, Abe, 186
Butterflies Are Free, 213
Buttons, Red, 186
Bye, Bye Braverman, 36, 38, 42, 43–46, 47, 53

Cabaret, 65, 210
Caesar, Sid, 186
Cahan, Abraham, 160–61
Call it Sleep, 103
Cantor, Eddie, 169, 186, 190–91
Capote, Truman, 75, 86
Capp, Al, 90, 93, 98
Carr, Vicki, 91
Carry Me Back to Morningside Heights, 68, 211–12
Carson, Johnny, 75, 80, 93, 194
Carter, Jack, 75, 83, 85, 186
Cavett, Dick, 89, 91, 93, 94, 98
Chamisso, Adelbert, 175
Chaplin, Charlie, 186
Chaplin's comedy (clash between privileged insiders and non-privileged), 22
Chassidism, 154–55
Chayevsky, Paddy (characters Italian or Irish, never Jewish), 35
Chewsday, 101
Child's Play, 217
The Chinese and Dr. Fish, 58, 213–14
The Chosen, 100
Chu Chem, 210
City Lights, 188
Civilization and its Discontents, 112
Clark, Dave, 216

INDEX

Cohen, Myron, 73, 77, 86, 186
Comedian, the Jewish: a cultural institution in American society, 185; the Jew and comedy officially married, 186; label of self-identity, the Jew as Jew, 194; professional exponent of the Jewish Comic Image, 185; set behavior role enables anyone to adopt it, 185; threadbare authenticity, nothing really Jewish about his "Jewish Humor," 194; work "shtik" used universally for comic bit, 185
Comic image of the Jew (comedy as a weapon against adversity), 145; in Germany, the Jewish nose, 179–80; cartoons, 179–81; echoes in creation of the Jew himself, 181
Comic Jewish Image: core in German Jewish humor, 163; in show business the very existence of the Jew is a major ingredient, 164; comicality grounded in social situation, 164; funny even to himself because he does not fit into the formal scheme of things, 164–65; approaches to, 168; the ultimate Image, 168
Comic Negro film image (overall not comic), 48
Comic stage Jew (three types): the foreigner, 65; the parent, 65; the *shlemiel*, 65
Comic "treatises" about Jews (a genre), 119
Conreid, Hans, 93, 98
Consciousness, mass, 13, 14, 15
Conversion to Christianity, movement toward, 139
Corey, Irwin, 186

Corio, Ann, 91, 94
Cosby, Bill, 71, 79, 87
Counsellor at Law, 49, 67
Criticism, fierceness of in Eastern joke, 150
Crossfire, 33
Cry for Us All, 217
Cultural lag in America: same Jewish Comic Image as that which originated among German Jews of the 19th century reflecting the absurdity of Jewish identity (self-irony), 199–200; not inherent in the social situation, 200

Dana, Bill, 76
Dangerfield, Rodney, 186
Davis, Sammy, 78, 87
Dawson, Richard, 74–75
Dayan, Moshe, 91
The Day the Whores Came Out to Play Tennis, 56–58, 207–8
Death of a Salesman, 52, 54
"Dejudaizing" characters, 16; Irving Shulman, 16; Arthur Miller, 16; Ben Hecht, 16–17
Don't Drink the Water, 210
Dubnow, 152

Eastern Europe (end of 18th century), 146–58; humor of "pious blasphemy," 150; parody of Talmudic logic, 150
East European Jewish immigration, 160
Eban, Abba, 100
The Education of Hyman Kaplan, 56, 212
Eliot, George, 144
Elkin, Stanley, 115
Ellington, Duke, 79, 87

Encounter: of son with Jewish immigrant father, 103; with American Jewish middle-class parent (more likely the mother), 104
The Engagement Baby, 58, 214
The Enlightenment, 136, 137; Jewish middle-class mutilated consciousness, 141
Erter, Isaac, 151
Ethnic conflict with environment (in *The Angel Levine*), 37
Ethnic humor, 22, 23; validity of, 23
The Exhaustion of Our Son's Love, 208-9

Father mortified by son, 58
Fiddler on the Roof, 56, 207
Films: "there are no serious films about the American Jew, but no cumulatively comic presentations of any other group," 47
The Firm Gets Married, 169
The Fixer, 37
Flora, the Red Menace, 208
Flying Nun series, 71
Foster, Phil, 186
"Foxy" Jewish inter-personal behavior, 89
Frederick the Great: interest in French culture, 136
Friedman, Bruce Jay, 104-9
Friends and Enemies, 208
Frost, David, 72, 74, 75, 79
Fuchs, Daniel, 123
Funny Girl, 37

Gabor, Zsa Zsa, 94
Garagiola, Joe, 81, 88
Generation gap, 159, 160
Gentlemen's Agreement, 33
German humor: grew out of flux; its mode self-expression, its purpose inner relief from social tension, 149
German Jewish humor, 163; questioned identity, 163; ultimate core of Comic Jewish Image, 163
Germany, birthplace of modern Jewish humor, 141
Ghetto life (in novels), 103
Gilford, Jack, 210
Gillem, Stu, 92, 96
Gleason, Jackie ("universal" point of view), 185
Gold, Michael, 103
Golden Rainbow, 211
Goldmann, 13
Golstein-Goldscheider (study of Jews in Providence), 18
Goodbye, Columbus, 37, 38, 40, 93
The Good Bye People, 56, 212
Gordon, J. L., 151
Graham, Billy, 97, 99
Graziano, Rocky, 80
The Great Dictator, 187
"Great retreat" in early thirties, 16, 33
Greenberg, Dan, 102
Greene, Shecky, 74, 78, 86, 186
Griffin, Merv, 73, 74, 75, 76, 77, 78, 79, 80, 86, 90, 91, 92, 94, 95, 96, 97, 98

Hackett, Buddy, 186, 207
I Had a Ball, 207
Harold and Sondra, 210
Harrigan, Edward, 162-63
Haskala (Enlightenment), 147; authors wished to build, not destroy, 151. *See* Enlightenment; Hebrew literature
Heaven Help Us, 112

INDEX

Hebrew literature, 147; in Germany, 147; in East Europe, 147; satire the mark of *Haskala* fiction, 149
Hecht, Ben, 16
Heine, Heinrich, 140, 141–43, 144, 150, 159, 162, 195
Henry, Pat, 81, 89
Herberg, Will, 18, 19, 85, 201, 202, 204
Herz, Henriette, 137
Herzog, 104
Hillel, 194
Hogan's Goat, 69, 215
Hope, Bob ("universal" comic point of view), 185
How to Be a Jewish Mother, 109, 211
Hughes, Howard, 79, 89
Humanist-rationalist notions of Jewish intellectuals, 146
Humoresque, 49
Humor of the cities, 159–71
Humor of Emancipation (2nd half of 18th century), 135–45; with movement of privileged groups into town, 135–36; movement of small German groups toward the French Enlightenment, 136
Humor of the Jewish Comedian, 185–96
Humor of Vaudeville: basis in superficial attribute of mispronouncing the native language, 161; presenting the ethnic type in America around 1900, 161–62; McLean's sociological study, 162

I Love You, Alice B. Toklas, 37, 38, 42
Image, denoting emotional and/or intellectual impact on a crowd, 12
The Impossible Years, 208
"In-group" atmosphere (of night club and Catskill hotels), 17
Inquest, 65, 214
Inside humor (TV), 82–84; inside remark, 87
Institutionalization of Jewish comic image: contradicts notion that the Jew has an identity to be taken as "seriously" as that of other Americans, 204; reinforces latent anti-Semitism, 204
Institutionalized jester: centuries ago in Jewish community life— the *badhken* or *marshallik*, 194; transformation from *marshallik* to Jewish comedian, 195
Institutionalized Jewish humor, 149; self-critical, 151
Irish Comedy, 47
Irving of Arabia, 102
Israel's Jubilation or the Birthday of the Great Contractor, 176
Is That You, Norman?, 58
Italian humor, 88
I Was Dancing, 215

Jacobi, Lou, 214
Jaffe, James (sociological study, *The American Jews*), 100
The Jazz Singer, 49
Jessel, George, 74, 79, 86, 186
The Jew a "front" for the American middle-class ethos, 58
"Jewish" as comical, 11, 12, 15–16; TV audience conditioned not to take the Jew seriously, 12; a stimulus to the response of laughter, 15, 16
The Jewish comedian (the only

explicitly Jewish role in the mass media): his style parochial, developed for limited and specialized audience, 17; spearhead of the Jewish return to the media, 17–18; central figure of the Jewish comic image, 18; a link to the humor of the Jewish past, 26; typically a "stand-up" comedian (honest, hearty, loving), 191; implicitly claimed honesty inherently tainted, 192; no longer a *Jewish* institution, but a creation of the popular culture, 195; social-psychological mechanisms at work in creation of, 195. See also Jewish Comic Image; Comic image of the Jew; Comic Jewish Image; Comic stage Jew; "In-group" atmosphere; Institutionalization of Jewish comic image

Jewish Comic Image: in America, historical background, 125–45; in Europe, 123–24; existence of, 197; American Jewish comedian the purveyor of, 197; Jewishness itself a comic prop, 171; institutionalization in the American media, 171; the Jew a gratuitously funny figure, 99; a Cosmic Clown, the essence of the Human Comedy, 115; urban antihero as a genre, 115; books the least effective propagators of, 119; important commodity in the theatre, 16, 51–70; the ideal-typical, 196; films meet almost perfect criteria for, 129; lingering "ethnicity" accountable for, 19–20; *See also* The Jewish comedian; Comic image of the Jew; Comic Jewish Image; Comic stage Jew; "In-group" atmosphere; Institutionalization of Jewish comic image

The Jewish Encyclopedia, 11, 12, 15, 19
Jewish "foxiness," 86
Jewish humor, collections of, 124; Salcia Landmann's *Der Jüdische Witz*, 124, 125, 130
Jewish identity a kind of automatic comic device, 50
The Jewish King Lear, 159
Jewish Mother, 60; suburban, 40, 41, 42, 47, 108, 109, 111; in *Portnoy's Complaint* a new culture monster, 109, 111
Jewish Nose, 173–74
Jewish Past, meaning and function of humor in, 20
Jewishness: risqué subject, 17; not really respectable in America, 19
"Jewish Renaissance," 16
"Jewish temperament," 42–43
Jewish writers of the thirties, 103
Jews Without Money, 103
Jimmy Shine, 212–13
Jokes from Germany (examples), 166–68
Jolson films (father-son relationship), 34
Jonah, 209
Judenschwein theme in Middle Ages, 172

Kaye, Danny, 169, 186
Kaye, Georgie, 186
Kazin, Alfred, 103
King, Alan (comedian-turned-rabbi-turned-comedian), 20, 208
Klassiker des Feuilletons, 144

INDEX

Kopit, Arthur, 56–58
Kracauer, Siegfried, 13
Kraus, Karl, 165
Kristol, Irving, 150, 155

Lahr, Bert, 186
Landmann, 149–50. 165; themes in her typology of the modern Jewish joke, 165
Last of the Red Hot Lovers, 214
Latency, 15
The Latent Heterosexual, 212
Laughter: of derogation, 198; of admiration, 198
Lawford, Peter, 77, 83
Lee, London, 186, 194
Leites, 13
Leonard, Jack E., 90–91, 98, 186
Lester, Jerry, 186
Levene, Sam, 209
Levinson, Sam, 76, 186
Lewis, Jerry, 186
Lewis, Robert Q., 186
Lieber, Joel, 115
The Little Man, 153–54
The Lost Weekend, 35–36
Lowenthal, Leo, 13
Lubitsch, Ernst, 168–69; introduced "sophisticated" comedy to Hollywood, 169
Lukacs, 13
Lumpenbourgeoisie, quality inherent in (opposition of Hebrew and Yiddish, of sacred and profane), 157; comedy of a problematic identity to become the mark of the city Jew, 158

MacRae, Gordon, 91, 98
Maimon, Salomon, 137–38
Marching Song, 67
Marjorie Morningstar, 102

Martin, Dean, 80
Martin, Tony, 73, 81, 82–83
Marx Brothers, 215
Marx, Groucho, 186, 188
Marx, Karl, 140
Mason, Jackie (essentially "religious" humor), 20, 186, 213
Mass media: reflect and in turn reinforce public opinion, 13. *See also* Media
Matty, the Moron, and the Madonna, 69, 215
McMahon, Ed, 93
Meara (of Steller & Meara), 92, 98
Media, 12, 13, 17, 20, 21, 24, 31–33, 51; films, 33–50; theatre, 51–70; television, 71–99; books, 100–120; Jewish return to, 17; study of, 20
Mendele, the Bookseller (pseud.), 153
Mendelssohn, Moses, 136–39, 146
Meyer Becomes a Soldier, 169
Meyer on the Alps, 168
Michener, James, 100
Middle-class parent, a target, 58
Mike Downstairs, 216
Miller, Arthur, 16; *The Price,* 52–55; *All My Sons,* 52; *Death of a Salesman,* 52
Minnie's Boys, 215
Minor Miracle, 215–16
Mintz, Eli, 208, 213, 215
Mirsky, Mark, 114
Money-lending motif, 174
Monopoly, 210
Morgan, Henry, 186
"Mother-in-law" jokes, 22
A Mother's Kisses, 108
Move!, 115
Murray, Jan, 76, 186

My Fair Sadie (temple musical in Heaven Help Us), 113
My People, 100
My Rabbi Doesn't Make House Calls, 101

Nathan Weinstein, Mystic, Conn., 209–10
Negativism in Jewish self-evaluation, 89
New Yorker, 111
Nicholas I, 148
No Greater Love, 49
Non-comic depiction of American Jews (in films of the twenties and early thirties), 49
Non-Emancipation humor, 146–58; satire the mark of Haskala fiction, 149
Norman, Is That You?, 214
Not a Way of Life, 216
No Way To Treat a Lady, 36, 38, 41

O'Brien, Pat, 92, 96, 98
The Odd Couple, 36, 38, 40, 42, 60, 61, 72, 207
Odets, Clifford, 34
Oliver, 37
O'Sullivan, Maureen, 94–95
The Other Man, 65, 211
Ostropoler, Hershele (Jewish prankster of the 18th century), 131

Packwood, Senator Bob, 94, 98
Pallenberg, Max (pre-Hitler German comedian), 164
Paris Is Out, 214
Parkyakarkis, 186
Partisan Review, 43
The Pawnbroker, 36
Peck, Fletcher, 186

Peerce, Jan, 93–94, 98
The Penny Wars, 65, 213
Phaidon, 136–37
Photoplay, 75; reporter, 83
Picon, Molly, 211
Pig the symbol of the taboo for the Jew, 173
Play It Again, Sam, 59, 60, 61, 212
The Pocket Watch, 209
Polls, 13, 14, 15; American Jewish Committee, 14
Popkin, Henry, "The Vanishing Jew of our Popular Culture," 16, 17
Popular culture (mass media) study, purposes of, 21
Portnoy's Complaint (the hero's name is a "code" word), 31, 102, 119; Portnoy's gags take the place of insight, 106
Potash and Perlmutter, 49, 66, 169
Potok, Chaim, 100
Powdered Eggs, 115
Predicaments, the four major, in films, 37–38
Pre-Emancipation period, 125–34
The Price, 52–54, 198, 211
Prince Sammy, 169
The Producers, 36, 38, 39, 46, 120
The Promise, 100
Pully, B. S., 75

Rabbi as comic, 41, 45–46, 47
Reiner, Carl, 77, 83
Reform rabbis, 76
"Religious" humor, 20, 45–46, 186
Rice, Elmer, 49
Rickles, Don, 186, 193–94
The Rise of David Levinsky, 160–61
Ritz Brothers, 186
Rivers, Joan, 90, 94, 98, 99
Rock, Monte, 97

INDEX

Rose, Biff, 97
Rosemary's Baby, 49
Roth, Henry, 103
Rothschild jokes, 149
Russell, Bertrand, 95
Russell, Mark, 75
Russell, Nipsy, 79, 87

Sahl, Mort, 186
Saphir, Moritz, 144
Satire, bitterness in, 151, 152; satirists turn to Yiddish end of 19th century, 152–53; already entrenched in popular sense of self-irony, 153; satiric point of view becomes domesticated in America, 169
Saturday Night, 212
Schiller's *Ode to Joy,* 150
Scuba Duba, 60, 61, 62–65, 210–11
Self-acceptance, 133
Self-image of the Jew (self-irony): militates against both the "respectability" of Judaism and his perfect Americanization, 200; a way of maintaining a sense of being Jewish, 201; best chance of survival of all Jewish traits, 201; most readily available tradition for reinforcing inner sense of group identity, 202; a distinctive Jewish possession, 203; fanned in America by show business and TV, 203
Self-questioning, 134
"Serious" American Jew a rarity on the American stage, 65, 68
Sex, sexuality, 107, 165
Shawn, Dick, 77, 186, 212
Sheen, Bishop Fulton, 80, 88
The *shlemiel* hero, 59, 60, 61, 62
Shoe Salon Pinkus, 169

Show Me Where the Good Times Are, 213
Shulman, Irving, 16
Sign in Sidney Brustein's Window, 65, 68, 207
Silvers, Phil, 186
Simmons, Charles, 115
Simon, Neil, 40, 207, 214–15
Skulnik, Menasha, 209, 210
Socialism, 140, 141
"Society for Culture and Science," 142
Sociology-of-literature tradition, 13
Some Like It Hot, 36, 60
Something Different, 60, 211
The Source, 100
Square in the Eye, 208
Stand-up comedian: a salesman at heart, 193; avowal of Jewishness meant as a form of confiding, a confidence *trick,* 193
Stang, Arnold, 186
Steam Bath, 217
Steffens, Lincoln, 159
Steinberg, David, 76, 87
Stern, 104–8
Storch, Larry, 186
Street Scene, 49
Sukenick, Ronald, 115
Summer in Williamsburg, 103
Susskind, David, 95
Symphony of Six Million, 49
Synagogues, increase of, 202; religion the official tag of the Jew in America (Herberg), but Jews *believe* the least, 202; with vacating American Jews the daily liturgy is not the Hebrew prayer but the comic monologue, 202

Talk shows (evening), 71; prepared comic monologue, 71

Talmud, humor in, 129
Tarr, Herbert, authentic comedy (*Heaven Help Us*) of suburbanite temple-goers, 112
A Teaspoon Every Two Hours, 58, 213
Television, 71–99; Jews given the most comic presentation, 99; humor based on assumption that Jewishness is funny, 99
That Summer, That Fall, 69, 216
Theatre (New York), 51; off-Broadway, 51; Broadway, 51
They Fought Back, 100
They Shall Not Die, 67
Thomas, Danny, 79
Thou Worm, Jacob, 114
To an Early Grave, 43
Toldoth Hachassiduth, 152
Tonight Show, 73, 75, 76, 77, 78, 79, 80, 81, 90, 91, 93, 94, 96, 97
Tornabene, Lyn, 102
Treacher, Arthur, 96
Tucholsky, Kurt (pre-Hitler German satirist), 164

Up, 115
Updike, John, 116–18

Vallee, Rudy, 92, 95, 98

Waiting for Lefty, 67
Walker, Betty, 77

Walking to Waldheim, 211
Welles, Orson, 91, 98
Welles, Patricia, 115
Werfel, Franz, 22
We, The People, 67
What's a Jewish Girl?, 102
A Whistle in the Dark, 217
White, Slappy, 79, 87
Wiesel, Elie, 100
Wilder, Billy, 35; audacity in his films, 36
Wills, Chill, 74
Winchell, Paul, 186
Winterset, 67
Winters, Jonathan ("Universal" comic point of view), 185
Wolfman, 13
Wouk, Herman, 102; *Marjorie Morningstar*, 34, 35; *Middle of the Night*, 35
Wynn, Ed, 169, 186

Yellow Jack, 67
Yiddish, 60; -speaking Negro, 60; speech patterns, 61; fun aroused by, 84, 85, 86; phrase placed judiciously for shock, 84
Yiddishe Mama, 109
Yiddish writers, 153; adopt comic pseudonym out of embarrassment, 153
Youngman, Henny, 186

The Zulu and the Zayda, 209